Journey to Love

PRAISE FOR *JOURNEY TO LOVE*

"The ultimate life changer in a child's life is a teacher or mentor. Christina was one such wonderful person. Her inspiration and ideals will live on forever in the lives she touched."

—Sylvia Weinstock

"*Journey to Love* will help you find inspiration in life. Christina Houri and I shared a common love for children and I had hoped one day to teach my dance program to her students. Christina opened her heart in more ways than one. Through her honesty, she teaches us not to make the same mistakes she did. Christina teaches us lessons such as looking twice before you jump and if you have a dream, do it now! Don't wait. Through her love for children, she found herself. Reading this book will help you discover your own path, whatever it may be."

—Pierre Dulaine, founder of Dancing Classrooms, subject and star of films *Take the Lead* and *Dancing in Jaffa*

FROM LIVING IN FEAR,
to Living in Faith

CHRISTINA HOURI

FOREWORD BY REEM ACRA

Published by Elsi Hakim, New York
www.livingthejourneytolove.com

Edited and designed by Girl Friday Productions
www.girlfridayproductions.com

Calligraphy by Ellen Weldon Design, LLC
Cover image: *O-Zone* © Pierre Marcel, 1995
Cover design: Rachel Christenson
All photographs © Elsi Hakim

ISBN (Hardcover): 9780998389424
ISBN (Paperback): 9780998389417
e-ISBN: 9780998389400

First edition

Printed in the United States of America

I dedicate this book to my mother, whose unconditional love and endless support helped me through my journey. To Oprah Winfrey, who made a profound impact on my life and inspired me to become more of a humanitarian. To all human beings who show courage when taking the spiritual path to become whole and reach their highest potential.

—Christina

To my son, Khalil, for seeing life through the eyes of God.

—Elsi Hakim

The need for another hovers over us,
unseen but majestic—a force field of emotion.
A solitary walk may turn into an encounter with
the most alien of creatures . . . Our self, naked,
expectant with hope, ready to abandon the beaten
path for the strange mystery of love.

—Jim Tommaney

Journey to Love

FROM LIVING IN FEAR, to Living in Faith

CHRISTINA HOURI

FOREWORD BY REEM ACRA

TABLE OF CONTENTS

My dear friend Tina Houri shared everything with me. And yet, she'd always say, "You'll understand me more when you read my book."

And she was right.

Now that I have read her book, the book you hold in your hands, I see that Tina was like all of us—in search of love, happiness, and home.

She left so much love wherever she went and in whatever she touched. In her journey, she learned that her search was for something much more important than a job or any tangible thing.

Tina was in search of her soul.

Once she found her true soul, she sent us all the lessons she learned along the way—all written here, in this book. Reading my friend Tina's words will guide you toward a better and easier life on Earth.

Tina shares her journey to teach us about our own little paradise, the world that surrounds us every day. She didn't realize that her journey was being written to guide us, and yet, with every word, she gave us that power.

I met Tina in 1984. We were both studying at the Fashion Institute of Technology (FIT). Tina was earning her associate degree in fashion design. I was a few years her senior, and one day I happened to be in the mail room when I saw a new mail slot that said "Christina Houri." I recognized the name as a Lebanese one, and being Lebanese myself, I looked forward to meeting her.

Tina happened to be walking by and reached in to get her mail. I said hello, asked if she was Lebanese (she said yes, and that she was part Greek and part Lebanese), and we started talking. We went to get coffee and quickly bonded. We introduced our mothers to each other; they also became fast friends. I am still close with Tina's mom, Elsi, who shares more of Tina's story in the epilogue of this book.

Tina and I remained good friends through the years. I admired so many things about her, but one instance in particular remains in my mind: how she handled loss.

During a difficult time in her life, her financial situation changed drastically. And yet, Tina didn't. She handled the negative change with grace, proof that possessions are not the key to happiness. We all know that, of course. Yet, by her actions, she showed how little she coveted material things. She didn't let the change get her down in any way. She never complained. She just kept on living her life with joy.

And that's only one of many instances during which I watched Tina *live* the principles she shares in this book. She practiced what she preaches. I am grateful to her for leaving us with her lessons, and I miss her deeply. I believe that even if you weren't fortunate enough to know Tina, you will know her after reading her words.

And that's fortunate for all of us.

Thank you, Tina, for this gift.

—REEM ACRA
NOVEMBER 2016

My best ME, the way I want to feel, always!

It was an autumn day
I remember that day in the park
Imagery of gold beauty
Surrounded us . . .
The sounds of leaves crackling under my feet
So crisp . . .
My field of vision entranced by a palette of colors
So vivid . . .
I could still hear the birds singing
Love songs to one another
For it was a day for expression
That day so clear to me . . .
Tranquility invaded my body and soul
Purity and serenity flew by me
The lake . . . a mirror of water
A little breeze transported me
Lifting me to places far beyond
That day comes back to me
Once in a while soothing my inner soul
Reminding me how beautiful life can be.

In this book I tell my story, the story of those experiences that pushed me to reach for my highest potential. I find it harder to connect to abstract ideas, but these experiences were truly lived. Yes, truly lived! My hope is that this telling will make my discoveries more tangible, more accessible to everyone.

You need to have two things in order to follow this path of self-realization: the will to grow and the courage to do it. I am blessed to have both. For what is life without a true purpose? What is life without trying to attain one's highest potential?

Throughout my early childhood and even into my twenties, I was a happy-go-lucky girl. I always tried to be the good girl, and I strived to please everyone around me. My parents sheltered me and my brother and gave us a good life. We rented a house on a different Greek island every summer to spend time with my Greek grandparents. Life as a family was wonderful.

Every couple years, my father's business moved us to a different country. We finally settled down in New York City, where I finished high school. When it came time to apply for college, I had to fight to pursue my creativity. My father wanted me to go to business school, but I wanted to go to a big university that offered both art and business classes. I ultimately got my way, and to appease my father, I took a few business classes. I studied very hard in these classes, yet I always got Cs on my tests. Meanwhile, in my art classes, I didn't have to study, and I got all As. Looking at these indisputable facts, I had to confront my father and tell him that my heart was

in design, not business. "There's no money in art!" he screamed.

But I shrugged off his concerns. After all, I had grown up with financial stability, and he and my mother had taken such good care of me that I had no concept of money and its value. All I wanted was to be happy. I aspired to be a fashion designer, but when I realized that in order to be successful I would have to become a workaholic, I changed my mind, opting for fun, low-paying nine-to-five jobs instead. I was simply not ambitious.

Ever since I can remember, I'd wanted my father to be proud of me. Yet in his eyes I knew that I had failed, because his idea of success was to earn a lot of money and work in a business environment. And even though my mother is also an artist, he simply did not understand the artistic world.

When my parents divorced, I decided to move far away—to try to escape the pain. I thought that only young children were impacted by their parents' divorce; I was in my midtwenties when that happened and I can assure you that it greatly affected me. I was mature enough to understand that two people can grow apart, but still it saddened me that it happened to my own parents.

For some people, life is a struggle. Perhaps God puts people through hardships as a test to give them a chance to become wise and whole. For some people it is a given—their talent is revealed to them at an early age. They are the lucky ones.

When I was seven years old, I wrote letters of the alphabet on little pieces of paper and stapled them together to make booklets. Then I lined up all my Barbie dolls. Each doll received a booklet, thereby becoming my student. Recalling how enthusiastically I played this game, I think that I was always meant to be a teacher.

Looking back on my life, I see that I have always had a passion to help people grow, to improve themselves, to reach their highest potential. I have become deeply connected to people, and I have tried to support them in whatever way I could. So I thought to myself, why not use a wider frame of communication to reach more people? Though there are many books on the subject, I hope that mine will be different. And that it will help others, no matter what paths they choose.

CHAPTER 1

Christmas on the slopes.

Snuggled in his arms
I feel secure
Like a child
In her mother's arms
Protected from all things
Life seems peaceful
Nothing in the world
Will ever separate us

Snuggled in his arms
I have nothing to fear
The beauty of life
Surpasses all the problems
Need of nothing
As long as I am
Snuggled in his arms.

I was not looking for love when I went to Colorado to visit a friend. I was just planning to ski and have fun, but my first night there, the universe threw a surprise my way.

I met Matt at a party, and we had an instant connection. I chose to ski with him instead of my friend, and though I felt terrible about it, I also felt like I just had to be with him during my short time in Colorado. On the day of my departure, Matt and I exchanged addresses, and I gave him three hundred dollars to help cover his rent. I had only known Matt for ten days, but that did not matter to me—I knew he was in need and I was happy to help. I was having feelings that I'd never experienced before, and I wished that Matt didn't live so far from New York. My heart sank when we parted at the airport.

A couple weeks later, I got a three-hundred-dollar check and a letter from Matt in which he thanked me and let me know that he'd decided to move back east to be closer to me and his family. I was thrilled by this news. After he arrived on the East Coast, we kept in touch, talking on the telephone a few times a week.

I went to visit him for Christmas. He lived in a cozy little cabin surrounded by mountains. In the living room, there was a large window with a view of the small lake across the street. He'd decorated the house in my honor and hung beautiful ornaments on a tall Christmas tree.

On New Year's Eve, Matt lit a fire in the fireplace. I put on a beautiful black embroidered gown that I knew he would like, and when I walked down the stairs into the living room, I could see Matt's eyes growing wide. "You look beautiful," he said breathlessly, with a big smile on his face. Though he usually wore clothing that reflected his down-to-earth personality—mostly sweatshirts, baggy jeans, and hiking boots—that night he'd also dressed for the occasion in shiny black shoes, black pants, and a hunter-green sweater that matched his eyes. He looked very handsome, his green eyes glowing with happiness.

Matt had set the table with candles, and he'd prepared filet mignon with mushroom sauce, rice, and a salad with a tasty vinaigrette dressing. He did not want me to do anything; I was impressed. Music played softly in the background as we ate, and everything was just perfect. After dinner, we moved to sit in front of the fireplace, where we talked for a while about the love we had for each other and how destiny had brought us together. Then he gave me my Christmas present: a pair of gold earrings, each one made out of three interlocking hoops. Tears came to my eyes—no man other than my father had given me jewelry before, and I'd heard that if a man gives a woman jewelry, it is a sign of true love. I was happy.

We continued to watch the fire, mesmerized by its beauty. Then Matt caressed my hand, and we turned to look deep into each other's eyes. Finally, we kissed. I started to unbutton his shirt, while he slowly unzipped my dress. We shed our clothes, piece by piece, and made love passionately by the fireplace. Afterward, we didn't want to leave our little love nest, so we covered ourselves with a blanket and slept, embracing each other and loving every minute of it.

The next few days were spent hiking, ice-skating, talking, laughing, and making love. Matt introduced me to his family. His mother, who had curly blonde hair, a sweet smile, and a shapely figure, was pleased to see her son so happy. His sisters and brothers were there as well; they'd traveled from various parts of the United States to be together. I was having such a magnificent time that I did not want to go back to the city.

But like all fairy tales, this wonderful trip had to end. I returned to New York, and Matt visited me a couple of times throughout the next few years. Together we'd walk around the city, though he did not like the big crowds on the streets; Manhattan can be overwhelming for a country boy.

He was my first true love. And he was an alcoholic. He called me in the middle of one night and said, "I drink a lot. I need help." So I looked in the yellow pages and found an Alcoholics Anonymous

center close to his town. Soon he began to attend meetings.

He opened my eyes to addiction. Since I did not do drugs or drink much, I was pretty naive, and I didn't know anything about alcoholism. I really had no clue. I did not struggle with addiction; in fact, I wanted to help addicts to see that life can be a beautiful oasis of love and security. And because I wanted to help Matt and to understand his behavior, I started to read more about it. One book on the subject stood out. The book was *Codependent No More*, by Melody Beattie, and from it I realized that I was a codependent person. I also learned that addictive personalities develop because of a lack of love, and I felt grateful that my mother gave my brother and me a lot of love.

Once I went to an Alcoholics Anonymous meeting with Matt, and it really shook me up. I was stunned to see that there are people who wake up every morning and battle this addiction. After listening to people talk about their struggles, about waking up every day with their addiction the first thing on their minds and desperately wanting to indulge in it, I could hardly believe it. And the addiction itself never goes away, so all they can do is change their thoughts and transform their negative addictions into positive ones. I quickly realized just how sheltered I was. To wrap my mind around it, I compared alcoholism to having a box of Godiva chocolates in front of me. When it comes to chocolate, for me it's all or nothing—either I don't eat any or I eat the whole box and get sick. Of course, the consequences of drinking too much are a whole lot worse than a stomachache.

I was innocent, and very much enamored with Matt. I had put him on a pedestal, and I would have done anything for him. After four years in our long-distance relationship, I decided that I wanted to take it to the next level, which meant that one of us would have to move. But Matt was not ready, and we broke up. Yet I still wanted to help him and to be with him, so I called him soon after our breakup and asked him if he would join me for group therapy. Much to my surprise, he agreed.

The Landmark Forum was a wonderful three-day program in which we explored our higher conscious-ness. Afterward, Matt and I were walking in Central Park, enjoying the day and in love with each other again, when suddenly he started to look around and shout hello to passersby. "Hey, I know you! I love you!" he called to a man walking by. We sat on a bench and gazed at each other, and he said, "I see my face in yours." I didn't understand what he was going through, and I don't think he did either. He'd seen himself in everyone—that is the ultimate love. Though that was what we had been investigating at the forum, it took me a year or so to grasp that Matt had been undergoing a spiritual peak experience. This is when the soul is connected to everyone and everything around it, and with this elevated con-sciousness, many people experience oneness with nature. Such an experience is life altering.

Matt had been so used to connecting to his dark side, to his addiction, and he'd been missing a part

of himself. When I delved into the true meaning of this event, I concluded that he saw the spiritual part of himself in me, because that is what I had offered him. He saw God in my love for him, my unconditional love that blinded me to the wickedness in his behavior.

I admired Matt for admitting his problem and getting help. He turned his negative alcohol, sex, and food addictions into positive ones, like exercise and faith. He also opened my eyes to something I had been oblivious to: my commitment issues concerning my relationships with men. I'd heard that we attract the mirror image of ourselves, but I did not understand the concept until later in life.

Our long-distance relationship continued on and off for a total of five years. When we broke up for good, I felt heartbroken for the first time in my life. I remember sobbing through the movie *Ghost*, because finally I understood what it meant to lose a loved one, and how devastating it could be.

◆ ◆ ◆

CHRISTINA'S THOUGHTS

❖ Life is a learning experience. Learn from everything that happens to you. Embrace the negative experiences of your life. Don't try to escape them. If you do, you will repeat them, but when you embrace them, you actually get to learn the lessons behind them.

❖   Take a mini vacation. It is a way to recharge while discovering new places. Return on a Saturday so that you have a day to unpack, sort the mail, and do the laundry. You will be more relaxed on Monday knowing that you have finished the chores.

❖   Write in a journal. Take a pen and start writing. Your goal can be three pages a day, or fifteen to twenty minutes. Do not stop to think. Even if you feel like you have nothing to say, just keep writing, and you will be surprised at the new ideas that pop out. This is called stream-of-consciousness writing, which digs deep into the subconscious.

❖   Find a form of exercise that's fun. There are tons of sports and activities. And if you enjoy it, you won't feel like creating excuses not to do it every day. Exercise has to make you happy in order for you to keep doing it.

❖   Dress up even if you are only going to the supermarket. Everyone in Europe is always dressed well. I am not saying that you should always wear a suit—a nice pair of pants with a cool shirt will suffice. Because when you look good, you feel confident.

❖   Simplify your life. I cannot say it enough. Simplify, simplify, simplify. Cut out all unnecessary activities, and don't be afraid to say *no* if you

have too much on your plate. Quit trying to please everyone, for doing so will eat away your own time for growth.

❖ Live in the present moment. You cannot be sitting down if you are standing up, right? You waste a lot of energy worrying about the future, so when you catch yourself worrying, say to yourself: *stop*. Then focus on what's happening.

CHAPTER 2

The Soul~Searching Years

One beautiful summer day
with Dad in Southampton.

What is the meaning of life?
I would really like to know
Would it be that the world revolves
Would it be that the human being travels
    everywhere?

Finding himself in the middle of everything
He rests not knowing what to do
He's lost
As vast as the world is
He would always find a place
Depending on his chance and his intuition
He shall follow the road
The road that will lead him to happiness
Bringing him good and evil
Why? Asking . . .
Trying to solve mysteries in my head
Wanting to know the answers
Deceived once again by reality . . .
Deceived once again by what I thought was love
Wondering, does he think of me?
Was I special to him or just a passing wind?
Pensive am I through this beautiful starry night
Amazed at how life evolves.

My spiritual journey began after that terrible break-up. As you can imagine, I was absolutely distraught. It hurt so much that I thought I was going to die. The pain was so strong that I couldn't do anything but walk around aimlessly, tears rolling down my cheeks. Some days I cried so much that I felt like my insides were going to burst!

Until my relationship with Matt, I was innocent, naive, and very sweet. So, of course, I attracted a lot of playboys, a lot of sweet-talking, charming young

fellows who I thought would love me dearly and one day marry me. But by the time I broke up with Matt, I'd learned a thing or two. It was as if a veil had been lifted from my face, my innocence lost.

During the forum, I'd become aware that Matt was my father's type: the emotionally unavailable man. Most people unconsciously choose to marry someone like their parents in order to resolve their issues. But I did not want a man like my father.

I began to look for the opposite personality—the family man, a man who was kind, devoted, and sensitive—but my motives weren't necessarily pure. I noticed that nice guys were interested in me, and I was glad that I finally had some confidence. I dated a couple of nice guys, and it was fantastic. If I told them to go left, they went left; if I told them to go right, they went right. I was no longer a doormat—they were! All of a sudden, the tables had turned—I could manipulate and control men, and I was excited by it. I had POWER! Ah! Revenge is sweet . . .

At a certain point, I realized that I'd have to forgive my father for abandoning me if I truly wanted to heal my wounds. I thought it was interesting that losing Matt coincided with wanting to reconnect with my father. Exploring my subconscious had obviously been a very powerful experience, because after five years of not speaking with my father, I picked up the phone and dialed his number. As soon as I heard his voice, I told him that I loved him and burst into tears. That day, we talked for a couple hours—we had so much to catch up on.

I was living with my mother, proud to have only five boxes and three suitcases. That way, it was easy for me to just pick up and go. I'd grown up moving from one country to another every couple years, and this pattern of continual movement had been instilled in me. So the notion of buying furniture was inconceivable to me. My friends told me that it was not a big deal and that later I could always sell whatever I bought, but I was proud to have only a few things to my name. I was like a gypsy. I loved traveling and exploring the world. When a friend suggested that all my traveling might be a way to avoid what was really going on, I did not understand her, because I did not see my wanderlust as a desire to escape. I believed I was simply a free spirit who liked to travel. However, after I'd moved a couple of times, I realized that my problems were the same wherever I went. Then I understood that I needed to deal with my problems at once; otherwise, I would go on chasing a fantasy.

So I decided to stay, at least for a little while. I was unemployed and had a lot of time on my hands. To make matters worse, it was winter, and a very cold one, I might add. I needed *something* to help get me out of my misery. I'd always been interested in psychology, in what makes people do the things they do, and how our childhoods affect us as adults. So I began to read a lot of books on the subject. I also took up yoga, which was becoming popular in New York City. Apparently all the stresses of the city were taking a toll on its inhabitants; everyone was looking for some serenity and relaxation, and many people

had found yoga. I picked up the excellent *Acu-Yoga,* by Michael Reed Gach, which shows positions that relieve various aches and pains.

Yoga changed not just my body but my whole being. I started having peak experiences, in which I would feel like I was in touch with the spiritual world. One day, I was watching television when I looked out the window. On the building across the street, I saw a huge face that extended three stories high. It was a man's face: opaque white, with strong, chiseled features. I didn't make anything of it, and soon my eyes wandered back to the television. After a few minutes, I looked out the window again and there he was, still looking at me. I really had no idea who or what it was.

The following week, I went to visit a friend in Wyoming. It was much colder there than in New York, and snow covered everything. From my bedroom window, I had a sweeping view of the Tetons. On the bedside nightstand was a book about angels. I began to read it, and I was astonished to find the exact description of what I had seen the week before. I realized that, during a time of great despair, heartbreak, and confusion, an angel had come to comfort me!

From then on, I put my psychology books aside and started reading spiritual ones. I was consumed by them, hungry for anything pertaining to that subject. The first book I read that propelled me onto the spiritual path was James Redfield's *The Celestine Prophecy.* That book made me think more about energy and the universe. Though I'd begun reading these kinds of books to understand Matt, I ended up learning a lot about myself. The saying "He who helps others, helps himself" is absolutely true.

Back in New York, I continued to practice Phoenix Rising Yoga, a gentle yet strong practice focused on connecting with the divine. During the relaxation period at the end of these strenuous yoga classes, I started having visions. Afterward, the teacher would encourage us to share our observations, and I was always the one who'd had peak experiences. In one of my visions, I was standing in front of a waterfall, with Matt looking my way. I heard a voice saying, "He's not going to hurt you anymore." When a woman in the class said, with frustration in her voice, that she wanted to have such experiences, I realized I had a natural spiritual communication that I could tap into more easily than others could.

One day, I was lying on the mat, deep into relaxation, when I smelled trash. *This stinks*, I thought. *Somebody must have forgotten to take out the trash.* But I had not smelled it during the exercises. This odor would come back to haunt me a couple of times in relaxation during the yoga class, over a period of a few months. And I never understood the reason why!

I meditated with my eyes closed and my attention on the third eye, and soon I started to see colors. They just came to me. To understand their meaning, I read that they are actually connected to the chakras that are open. I found out that there are a total of seven chakras. The lower three chakras are said to be fear based, the upper three chakras spirituality based. The heart chakra, which is green and

in the center, is very important because it regulates our spiritual energy. So from then on, I knew that when I saw green and purple (signifying the fourth and sixth chakras), it meant that I was balanced. If, on the other hand, I saw orange and yellow (signifying the second and third chakras), it meant that I was having a bad day spiritually and that I was unbalanced.

To empty my head, I used to take long walks and, after an hour, collapse on the grass in Central Park. Lying down, I started to sense tingling in my legs, like a strong electrical current. Sometimes I even heard POP! . . . POP! I was baffled and wondered what was happening to me. When I asked my yoga teacher about it, he told me that it was the release of stress and nervous energy. Later on, as I became more relaxed and secure in life, the tingling disappeared.

One glorious day, I decided that I'd had enough suffering over the breakup. I went to the yoga class, and during relaxation at the end of the class, I heard a sound like *VOUM* and saw Matt's face. In my mind, I told him that I was kissing him for the last time, and then I heard *VOUM* again. Later that week, while browsing in a bookstore, I opened a book that, coincidentally, was about spiritual travels, and there I saw an explanation of the experience I'd had. It is called "soul traveling." And the strangest thing was that after that experience, I didn't suffer anymore, at least not about Matt. It was as if the spirit-to-spirit tie Matt and I shared had been cut, and I could start living again!

While all of this was going on, I was sending hundreds of résumés to large corporations, thinking that was the way I could become responsible like everyone else. By getting a good, respectable job, climbing the corporate ladder, and earning a decent salary, finally my life would be set and I would prove myself to my father. But my heart was just not in it, and even though I tried very hard to seem interested during the interviews, it might as well have been written on my forehead: "I do not want this job." So I did not land any.

One day, I remembered that Matt's mother had seen me playing with her grandchildren, and she suggested that I would be a good kindergarten teacher. Me, teach? I did not know how; I did not have a degree; I was rarely even around children! Yet despite my reservations, I looked in the yellow pages and found five preschools in the city. I began to send out résumés, assuming that nothing would come of it. At the same time, I was also seriously considering finding a furnished apartment to rent in Miami and looking for a job there.

Much to my surprise, a couple weeks later, I got an interview at a French preschool. When I arrived, I found a very colorful classroom, with plenty of educational materials on shelves around the room. The interview was mostly hanging around with the class—I'd never been with that many kids in my whole life! I noticed that I was very relaxed, that I was simply enjoying my interactions with the children. I even got invitations to some of the children's

birthday parties, which, in my mind, meant that I had passed the test.

I recognized that I had a natural ability to nurture and connect with children, and I left the school that day with a big smile on my face. The director must have thought the same thing, for the next morning, she called to let me know that I had gotten the job. As soon as I hung up the phone, tears of joy came streaming down my face. I was ecstatic. How did I get the job with no previous experience, you ask? Because I was truly engaged and passionate about what I was doing. So I did not move to Miami after all.

In my free time, I started taking evening classes on education and child development, and volunteering with underprivileged children. The group of volunteers would pick up kids from shelters in Harlem or the Bronx, and then take them on educational and recreational field trips and provide them a safe environment in which they could relax and enjoy the day. I became particularly attached to Jeremy, an eight-year-old boy with five brothers and sisters, who was taking care of his baby sister at night while his mother worked. He was skinny and tall for his age, and I was impressed by his maturity. Even though his mother did not have money to buy him new clothes, he was always properly dressed. During the week of Valentine's Day, he gave me a bracelet that he'd made with colorful beads, which I still keep in my jewelry box. I was very touched by his gift.

A couple weeks later, he did not show up for our meeting. When I asked the shelter about him, they informed me that his mother had passed away from an overdose. Jeremy's aunt had told him and his brothers and sisters that their mother had fallen out of bed and hit her head. With that news, my heart sank. Jeremy was so affectionate and caring, and he loved his mother dearly. What would become of these kids? Sadly, I never saw Jeremy again.

I was also part of a program that helps six- to twelve-year-old kids build self-esteem through modalities of therapy and play, which encouraged self-expression, group participation, and individual confidence. I loved spending time with these children and watching them grow. As much as I tried to give them a sense of hope for their future, they also gave me the hope I needed to go on with my life.

One evening, at a party, I was talking to a group of businessmen. When they asked me about my profession, I replied, "I am a teacher," with a big smile on my face. But all I got was: "Oh! That's cute." I was disgusted. I quickly found another group of people to talk to. This time, the group was composed of artists. When I told them that I was a teacher, their eyes grew wide and they began to rave about teachers and how inspirational they are. Quite a contrast, don't you think?

Teaching was a breath of fresh air after what I had gone through. Everybody was telling me that I looked radiant. After a year of misery, happiness had welcomed me with open arms! I said to myself that I did not need a man to be happy. Singing fun

songs with the kids, finger painting, playing games, learning the alphabet, running in the playground— all of it connected me to my childhood days. I found love and happiness once again. I never missed a day; even when I was not feeling well, I still went to school. The parents were pleased to see that their children were enjoying the class. I finally had a passion for something!

Those two years of teaching were the happiest of my professional life.

I'd thought I'd found a job that would last forever. Unfortunately, when I learned just how low a teacher's salary is, and without any real possibility of an increase over the long term, I had to recognize that this was not a feasible dream. In my opinion, there is nothing more important than having dedicated teachers to educate the next generation. I hope that one day someone in government will take notice and make changes. To this day, every time I remember those teaching years, I sigh . . .

So I had to find an alternative.

◆ ◆ ◆

I moved to Paris, France, for what was supposed to be a few months to "find myself" but ended up living there for a year. At that point, I hated men. I was angry and disgusted by men's selfishness, and I became somewhat of a male basher. There I hit rock bottom again, swirling down into a deep depression and, for the first time, experiencing thoughts of suicide. *What is there to live for, if I don't have a purpose or a husband to cherish or children to raise?* My hands and feet were sweaty all the time from anxiety. I used to sit in a bubble bath, trying to relax, but as soon as I got out of the bath, my hands and feet would be clammy once again.

I did not have any direction in terms of a career. I thought if I could only meet my soul mate, my misery would end, and everything would be all right. I am not a religious person, but I found myself going to a small church nearby and praying from the bottom of my heart for my soul mate.

A year later, I received a notice for jury duty in New York, which I had previously postponed three times. So I had no other choice but to go back and serve. In a way, I felt it was the jury duty that saved me from staying stuck and depressed in Paris.

Back in New York, I started looking for a job. Luckily, there was a position available in a small company, and I was hired right away. It was a fun group of people whom I was working with, and I was in great spirits again and having a wonderful time. My life was finally back on track.

◆ ◆ ◆

CHRISTINA'S THOUGHTS

❖   Please, please, please . . . whatever you do, raise your children to have *self-esteem* and *confidence.* Teach them to be the best they can be. Encourage them to reach for the stars. I believe

this to be the core of a successful life. You will be giving them a gift that is worth more than anything you could buy.

❖ Watch only the television programs that you like. Don't waste a lot of time flipping through the channels, when you could be spending time with your children, playing games, or being productive.

❖ Find a cause that speaks to your heart and volunteer your time. If it is a cause that you are passionate about, then volunteering will not be something you *have* to do, it will be something you *want* to do.

❖ Stand on your head for a few minutes every morning. I mean it . . . you think I am joking? It seems difficult, but it is very easy, especially if you balance against the wall. Ask a yoga teacher how, and then practice at home. You can do it. This is a very important pose because it opens the seventh chakra, which connects directly to higher consciousness.

❖ When traveling by train, sit in the first or last car, which is usually less crowded. Leave the house on time; that way you arrive to the station on time, and everything will flow smoothly, giving you a more relaxed commute. It's much nicer to avoid rushing.

❖ Take bubble baths or hot showers. Even if you think that you don't have the time, ten to fifteen minutes is all that it takes.

❖ Write down "coincidences."

CHAPTER 3

Second Love

The inspirational tools that always make me smile.

Oh, Beloved
Can you hear my cries?
Come, I beg you
Leave your world behind
My heart aches
Longing for you
My body shivers at the thought of you
Beloved
Show your true self to me
Come and whisper soft words

Come and caress my sensuous body
Will my cries be enough for you to come
And envelop me with your fire and passion
Oh Beloved
Let's share our thoughts and dreams together
Come soon . . .

My prayers for a soul mate were answered when I met Steve.

It had been six long years since Matt and I had broken up, and, at a certain point, I had vowed not to fall in love again unless the man was *the one*. That way, I was sure to avoid going through a horrible heartbreak again.

Until Steve, I'd only had long-distance relationships and flings while on vacation in exotic places. It became very clear to me why my past relationships had all been long-distance ones: they were emotionally safe, and I did not have to deal with the everyday routine of a real relationship. I'd believed that perhaps a family life was not for me because I preferred excitement. Nice men bored me, but a man on a motorcycle with no life goals: that excited me.

Steve and I connected immediately. On our first date, we shared a bottle of soda and talked for endless hours, giggling and laughing. He was a bit taller than me, with short black hair and small green eyes. He always wore starched, ironed shirts that gave him a tidy look, and his muscular physique

suggested dedicated time spent at the gym. His face was handsome—but I could see sadness in it as well. I was living with my mother at the time, who luckily traveled a great deal for business, giving us the opportunity to spend some time together. For the first six months, I kept my heart guarded, and yet I felt carefree, loving every minute.

I could not believe that a man like Steve could get my attention and hold it. He had to be *the one*. He was very affectionate, sensitive, and extremely attentive to my needs, which was a change from the way playboys had treated me in the past.

One day, I had a major breakthrough. "I am not scared anymore!" I screamed. I had broken my pattern of noncommittal behavior, or so I thought. I told Steve that, in the past, I'd felt suffocated if a man called me more than three times a week. But Steve and I called each other twenty times a day, and we were colleagues, too!

From the moment I had that breakthrough, something changed with Steve and me. Here's the thing about commitment: the moment you commit, the universe helps you to stay on course. We both committed to each other and became supportive of each other in everything. It was amazing. We fed off each other and motivated each other: I motivated him to take classes related to his field so that he could advance in his career, and he motivated me to take computer lessons to become more tech savvy. I said to myself, "Ah! So that's what a real relationship is all about!" I liked the idea of having someone to bare my soul to, to share everything with, and with whom I could make plans for the future. All that was new to me.

I just loved every inch of that man. We had an indescribable passion. One Saturday afternoon, I felt inspired to decorate the bedroom with candles. That night our lovemaking was so passionate that we literally set the room on fire! In the middle of everything, the lampshade caught fire, and flames spread through the room. We ran to the kitchen and filled a few buckets with water and, thankfully, extinguished the fire. We looked around the room and started to laugh, amazed that nothing was damaged. I guess that day we knew just how hot we were.

Soon our souls became intertwined, and we began to have uncanny mystical experiences. I had never kissed anybody like I kissed Steve. He and I would kiss for hours, and it was during one of these passionate kissing sessions that together we had an out-of-body experience. Steve called it "dancing with the angels." Indeed, we were! It felt like our souls were kissing, and for the first time in my life, I felt *loved*, truly *loved*.

One day, we were meeting for lunch at our favorite spot near the river. Though there were two roads to get there, for whatever reason, we always took the same one. But that day I really felt like taking the other route, and when Steve arrived ten minutes later, I was shocked to hear that he'd also come that same way. We had become one spirit!

Another time, at one point during our lovemaking, my body began to twitch all over. I could no longer feel it—I was out of my body, somewhere in the

spiritual realm. So it was clear to me that we were two souls meeting in heaven. We both wanted that spiritual love connection to last forever.

One sunny autumn day, Steve picked me up to go to the mountains for a romantic getaway. The leaves were changing colors: their reds, yellows, and oranges lighting up the way. At a beautiful spot over-looking the valley, we parked and walked through the woods hand in hand, talking and laughing, feeling on top of the world. We sat on a rock and looked out over the valley as we ate the ham and Swiss cheese sandwiches that I had lovingly prepared, talking about everything that came into our minds. I had never felt so close to Steve as I did that day.

Soon after that romantic getaway, I discovered I was pregnant. When I thought back to the previous couple weeks, I remembered one particular time when Steve and I had made love. Afterward, he'd laughed with joy; his face lit up with happiness. It must have been that special moment.

I was brought up to believe that a woman should be married before having children, and I did not want to live in shame. As much as I wanted a family, I immediately decided not to keep the baby, and I thought it best not to tell Steve. When I met him to tell him about my decision, he looked at me and said, "I knew."

"How did you know?" I asked, surprised.

"I just felt it," he said.

Steve confessed that he regretted that I hadn't kept the baby, because it would have been created from our spiritual union.

Looking through my mail one day, I found an envelope addressed with familiar handwriting. It had been sent to the house I had lived in four years earlier, then forwarded on to my current one. It was strange, I thought, since usually the post office forwards mail for only one year. I tore open the envelope and read the card. It was signed by Matt. I could hardly believe it! Six years later, and Matt wanted to rekindle our relationship. He wrote that he still thought about me, and that because of me, he'd started going to church and had found Jesus. When I called him to thank him for the card, he was ecstatic, and to me it felt like I was talking to an old friend.

I told him that I was seeing someone and that it was serious. I just could not believe that he was still hung up on me after all those years. Nevertheless, it was too late for us. Shortly after our phone call, he emailed me to tell me that he was finally able to let me go. I believe that I was meant to receive the card at that moment, because he needed closure so he could move on. And as soon as he did that, the universe brought him the woman he was meant to be with. Three months after our conversation, he met his future wife, and soon they had a baby. I think a clean break is healthier for our souls. We are able to move on, instead of living with the hurt and memories of the past. I was happy to hear from Matt and grateful that I had Steve in my life.

A couple weeks later, Steve came to pick me up, and this time we drove not to the mountains but to the ocean. It was a beautiful crisp day. We walked along the beach, gazing out at the horizon. Since it was fall, there was nobody in sight, and I started running as fast as I could. Steve ran after me and caught me at the edge of the lifeguard station. We sat there peacefully, looking at the waves unfolding on the sand. When we got back to the car, it was like we had absorbed all the energy of the romantic day into our hearts, and we exploded into passionate lovemaking.

On a cold day that November, Steve and I were walking around the city. When we got to the public library, he pulled me inside, saying, "It's warmer in here." The building's interior was beautiful and grandiose, with marble floors and wide old-fashioned stairways. Steve led me to an empty hallway, turned to me and looked into my eyes, and took a long gift box from his pocket. "This is for you," he said, a smile on his face. I was so excited that I tore the wrapping paper and opened the box as fast as I could. My heart was pounding. It was a gorgeous gold bracelet, with heart-shaped designs forming its circle. I had tears of joy in my eyes. I will never forget that day.

During those months, it was as though Steve had finally come out of his shell. He looked much better, happier, and more relaxed. After a year of dating, I felt that it was time for our relationship to move to the next level, which meant moving in together. But I was afraid to bring it up, nervous that I would lose Steve if I did. So I meditated long and hard for one week. One morning, I woke up with a solution. I decided to move out of my mother's apartment and get my own so that it would be easier for Steve to move in with me. I started looking for a one-bedroom apartment and, in a matter of three weeks, found one, with a huge living room and separate dining room, on the top floor of an old building. The kitchen window overlooked a small park. It was perfect.

Right before the move-in date and my birthday, I woke up at five in the morning to Steve's voice saying, in my mind, "It's going to be okay." It was very strange. When I told him about it, he did not sound surprised. He said, "That day, I kept saying 'it's going to be okay' in my heart over and over." When I researched this phenomenon, I found out that such an experience is called "transparent communication"—communication between two souls in the spiritual realms, which was what we'd done!

I took a week off from work so that I could organize my new apartment. A friend had told me about feng shui, an ancient Chinese philosophy that works with energy fields, and I'd bought the book *Lillian Too's Easy-to-Use Feng Shui*, which I encourage you to read because it is quite interesting. From its colorful illustrations and simple explanations, I learned more about the philosophy and how to arrange the furniture for optimal energy flow. The colors I chose were light and the layout of the furniture very simple. Every furnishing in the apartment was something that spoke to me. *Now*, I thought, *I have become a fully committed person*. After all, I'd moved out of my mother's apartment and even bought furniture! Plus, I had a job with a good salary, and I was able to pay the rent. I'd done it all for Steve. I took all of

this as a sign that he was my soul mate and that we were going to live happily ever after.

My mother came to visit and said, "It looks as if you are living in Florida." I'd always wanted to move to Miami, but somehow the years had passed and I just felt stuck in New York. So instead, I'd brought Florida to New York.

At that time, I felt Steve starting to pull away. Eventually this turned into a breakup. I was excited about my independence but sad because Steve was not with me.

My birthday came shortly after the move. The morning of my birthday, a colleague of mine called to let me know that a beautiful bouquet of long-stemmed red roses had arrived at the office. The sender had not revealed his name.

It had been a month since Steve and I had broken up, and I did not have any secret admirers that I knew about, so I gathered that the flowers were from him. I took the train to the office, because I could not wait to have the roses in my possession. My heart was pounding when I opened the card. It read: "The past strengthens you and the future is divine." I called Steve to confirm that it was his gesture. When I heard his voice, my heart skipped a beat. He told me that he loved me very much, that he was sorry, and that he would move in with me the following weekend.

I felt like flying. I was so happy that I went to a Hallmark store to look for a card. I found one with *Thank You* elegantly inscribed in silver. In the center of the card, I wrote:

Dear God:
Now I can smile because my soul mate
will be with me.

I sealed the envelope, and wrote:

To: God
Address: Heaven

With a big smile on my face, I ran to the nearest mailbox and pushed the envelope into the slot. My philosophy is always to be grateful—and grateful I was!

Saturday morning, I called Steve, but his cell phone was turned off. I waited an hour and tried again without success. The day passed without a word from him. That's when I knew that Steve did not have the courage to leave his wife and children.

Yes, Steve was married.

Steve had married young, to someone he was not in love with, to please his parents. It was almost like an arranged marriage. A couple years later, he realized his mistake. And I had never dated a married man before. Once, when I was working at a hotel, I met a very good-looking and charming soccer player who was on tour with his team. We started to flirt, then we kissed for a while, and then he asked me to go back to his room. On the way there, he told me that he was married and had two kids back in his hometown. I immediately stopped walking, turned around, and said, "You're married! Then I am not going with you." He was disappointed, of course, but

for me, it was inconceivable that I would go out with a married man. The next morning, he came to see me to apologize for what happened, and he told me that he admired my good morals.

I'd developed these morals the hard way—when my father's then girlfriend broke up our family, I was devastated. I hated her, and I said to myself that I would never do such a thing. Little did I know that a few years later, I would find myself in her shoes.

When I started the relationship with Steve, it did not bother me that he was married. But I wanted to understand why I was now okay with being in a relationship with a married man. Was Steve truly my soul mate, or was it just an affair? I went to the bookstore to find a couple of books on the subject. I was saddened by what I read, because it sounded a lot like our relationship. And I also read that having affairs is rooted in low self-esteem. *I don't have low self-esteem, so it must be Steve's issue,* I said to myself. I thought since I was controlling and assertive, I must have plenty of self-esteem, but to my dismay, I realized that those behaviors actually serve to hide low self-esteem. I also read the chapters about the possibility of staying married after an affair. I read them because, in my heart, I did not want his marriage to survive. I wanted him to love me and only me.

Before Steve met me, he'd never cheated on his wife. When I arrived on the scene, their marriage was already rocky. Steve had spoken to a lawyer about divorce, and he poured his heart out to me about his miserable family life. I became his confidant. He told me that his wife didn't give him the attention he wanted, and I felt pity for him. Deep down, he was angry at his circumstances, and though he didn't say it, he was pleading: *Save me, save me.* That's what I'd heard, loud and clear. He was so gentle, so kind and loving. Why would his wife not want such an endearing man? The difference between his marriage and his relationship with me was that it was not out of obligation that he spent time with me—it was because he was in love.

So it wasn't until the move that he showed any signs of apprehension. I believe that in his heart, he truly wanted to move in with me. And so I was devastated that night. My whole body trembled from shock, and at one point I could not breathe. I went to the emergency room, where the doctor gave me tranquilizers, and then I went home to sleep it off.

For days after, I called Steve again and again to get an explanation, but he'd changed his cell phone number and no longer worked at the same company. I had no way of getting in touch with him, so I kept on hoping and praying. I desperately wanted my soul mate back.

The following couple months, I became very depressed. I felt like I could not go on—I honestly don't know how I got through it. I was not used to drinking, but I took shots of cognac before going to bed to numb the pain so I could sleep. When I did sleep, I would do so with my arm extended to the other side of the bed, reaching out for Steve. Many nights I woke up, my body shivering and my soul screaming with anger and pain. Neither my body

nor my soul could accept his withdrawal. I felt like my life had no meaning anymore. I'd made plans with Steve and, just like that, everything had fallen apart. How could that be? It was not possible. *Life* was not possible without my soul mate. I cried and cried, deep in despair. What I feared had happened once again: I had to go through a painful breakup. "Why?" I kept asking God. "Why, after all my prayers, would you send me my soul mate only to take him away?"

A couple years earlier, I had broken up with a French man whom I had been seeing for a while. I found a healer named Max to disconnect our souls so that I could become a free spirit once again. During the session, I had a vision of the French man walking away from me and heard a voice saying: "He's not for you." I did not suffer much after that, glad that I had not put a lot of hope into the relationship. But when I went back to see Max so that he could disconnect my soul from Steve's, I had a different kind of vision. Steve was standing in front of me, and the voice I heard said: "You will see him again." But I did not want to see him again! Our story was finished.

When I walked around the city, everywhere I looked reminded me of Steve and the happy times we'd shared. I read Steve's name in everything, saw his face everywhere. I loved his cologne, so I went to perfumeries to find scents like his. It is a mystery to me how a fragrance can bring us right to the person who wore it! I even ran after a couple of men, thinking they were Steve. It was excruciating. Since

I never had a boyfriend living in the same city, I had not experienced such a thing.

During this period, every now and then I would feel a tingling on my forehead, which in spiritual terms is known as the third eye, considered the seat of intuition. One day, while I was in my office, my best friend called to ask me for a favor. It was raining, and I had no plans to go out for my lunch hour. She asked if I could pick up something for her and drop it off at her office. I was none too happy about the idea of walking around in the rain, and at first I resisted, but then I agreed. *Might as well be a good friend,* I thought to myself.

Before leaving the office, I started to feel that tingling on my forehead. This time, the sensation was very strong. I picked up what she wanted and was walking toward her office. I'd wanted to take another street, but for some reason I kept on walking the same way. Then I turned my head to the left, and who should I see but Steve, walking ahead of me. I had to do a double take, since I had been seeing his mirage everywhere. However, this time it was really Steve. It had been ten weeks since his disappearance. I called out his name. When he turned around and saw me, a surprised expression came over his face. We sat down in the park to talk, because he had some serious explaining to do.

He told me that he'd been all packed and ready to come to me that day when his son had an epileptic seizure. Steve had to take him to the hospital, and after the incident, he did not have the heart to

leave him. He realized that he was obligated to his family, and so he needed to stay.

"Did you have to change your phone number and leave me in the dark?" I asked. He replied that his wife had confiscated his phone and changed the number. He could have called me from anywhere, but he was afraid to get in touch with me, knowing how upset I must have been. He knew that his behavior was wrong. Steve told me that he was very confused, and that he'd been seeing a therapist to understand what was happening to him.

"I never stopped loving you," he said, his voice breaking. "I even kept a locket of your hair in my pocket to remind me of you." He gave me the name of the new company where he was working. After his explanations, I forgave him and agreed to meet the next afternoon. I thought there would be no harm in talking to Steve because I was planning to leave for France soon.

We met at a café downtown. Steve and I gazed at each other all afternoon while sipping our tea. He told me that he drove to the mountain spot where we had gone together. His soul had searched for mine all day. He walked the same path, sat on the same rock, and wallowed in his misery. On a tree, he inscribed my name to be forever lasting. I realized how much he truly loved me, how brokenhearted he was by the situation. He also informed me that, during our breakup, he went to a meeting and the two people conducting the meeting had our exact names! Such a crazy coincidence, we both thought. After reading books about synchronicity and coincidence, I later understood that whatever we put our attention on, we manifest. Years ago, I went out with a German man who liked the cartoon character Popeye. And believe it or not, during the couple months that we dated, I saw Popeye on T-shirts, on cars, basically everywhere I looked. But as soon as we broke up, I stopped seeing Popeye. Strange, I know, but that's how the universe works!

After tea, Steve walked me to the train station. His clammy hand squeezed mine every few minutes. He was nervous and knew that the end was near and that he was going to lose me forever. We embraced while waiting for the train, my body bound to his, tears streaming down my cheeks. "I love you," he said, emotion in his voice. I did not want to leave him, but then my train arrived. We said our good-byes; our gazes locked. I took a seat near the window, my heart feeling wretched. It was one of the hardest moments I had ever experienced. The train departed and, with it, my past.

The next morning, Steve called me. His voice was hoarse, as if he could barely speak. "How did you feel last night?" I asked him.

"I was happy," he replied.

"Then why don't you do something about it?" I asked.

"I don't know," he answered sadly.

We left it at that. I took a taxi to the airport. I was waiting with my carry-on suitcase at the gate, trying to call a friend, angling my phone this way and that to get some reception, when it rang. I thought it was my friend, calling to wish me bon voyage. To

my surprise, it was Steve. He had no idea what time my flight was departing and was lucky to catch me, since I was taking the last plane at eleven o'clock. His voice sounded angry.

"Where are you?" he asked.

"I am at the gate. The plane is leaving soon," I said.

"Get out of there," he said. "I am coming to pick you up."

I could not believe it. Why does it always take losing someone to know how much we care and to get the courage to do something about it?

I waited for him outside at Departures. My whole body was shaking. I felt as if I had won the lottery. After a while, Steve sped up the ramp and stopped the car in front of me. He opened the door and ran into my arms, hugging me with all his strength, my body still shaking from the excitement. "I love you," he said. "I want to be with you, I want to go home." Those few words meant the world to me. His courageous act, his passion for me, all unfolded like a scene from a romantic movie.

He'd brought a small suitcase. We drove back to my apartment, where I still kept a closet empty for him, as well as a few shelves for his books. We sat down on the sofa, looking out the window. "I feel so comfortable here, I love it," he said with a big smile on his face. He opened his arms and shouted, "Ah! A new life!" We opened a bottle of champagne to celebrate.

That night, we were so excited to be together that we didn't sleep a wink. We went to bed and held each other, looking into each other's souls. So much passion, so much love poured out through our wide-open eyes. We were going to be together forever, and nothing and no one was going to tear us apart.

The next afternoon, Steve called his wife to tell her that he was going to pick up the rest of his things. He also called his parents to let them know that he was fine and to ask them not to try to convince him to go back. I gave him a couple suitcases and the key to my apartment. He told me that he would be back in a couple hours. Nine o'clock came and went and still he had not returned. I started to worry.

I called Steve to ask him where he was, but his cell phone was off. I waited anxiously. An hour later, he appeared on my doorstep. When I opened the door, a man was standing next to him. The man just stood there, not saying anything, while Steve handed me my empty suitcases. He told me that he could not stay, that he was very sorry and to for-get about him. His body language showed me that he was very nervous, afraid even. He was not the same man who'd been with me in my apartment the night before, a man full of love and happiness. My imagination started running wild, and I thought that his family had sent this other man as some kind of escort to make sure that Steve went back to them. I thought Steve was their prisoner. Without even a good-bye, he ran down the stairs as fast as he could, with the mysterious man right behind him.

Just like that, he'd left. I was livid. He'd made me give up my airplane ticket for nothing! He'd done it to me again!

The following week, I called him at work. My voice shaking with anger, I told him that I wanted the money lost on that plane ticket. He agreed to pay for it, but I doubted that I would ever get that money back. He proceeded to explain what had happened. Apparently, when he'd finished packing his things, his son had thrown a tantrum and his wife had started guilt-tripping him for leaving them.

I forgave him once more and agreed to meet the next day. He came to pick me up at work, and we ran into each other's arms. We hung on to that hug as long as we could, happy to be together once again. In that moment, it felt as though the strength of our love could overcome all obstacles. Yet soon I would find out just how true the saying "Love makes you blind" really is.

Steve said, "Come on, I want to take you someplace." We walked for a while, finally stopping in front of a church. We entered the church hand in hand. The chapel walls were a dark wood, giving it a somber ambiance. "I would like us to pray together," Steve said. When he saw me close my eyes to pray in silence, he shook my hand and told me to pray out loud, so that he could hear me. I had never prayed that way before and felt his request was a sign of codependency. In our prayers, we thanked God for bringing us back together again and wished he would help us stay together for many years to come.

We clasped hands tightly as we left the church. I felt as if I had just gotten married, that now we were going out into the world as husband and wife. It was a weird feeling that gave me goose bumps.

Despite our prayers, Steve could not muster the courage to leave his children. We talked on the phone a few times, and then I decided to let him go so I could move on with my life. He was being selfish by leading me on, and I could not live in limbo anymore. I have heard that some women stay with a married man for years, hoping that someday he will leave his family. I wanted to have a family of my own, and my biological clock was ticking, and I was certainly not going to waste my whole life waiting.

I could not believe that Steve turned out to be an addict just like Matt. He was very affectionate with me, and I thought calling me twenty times a day was simply a sign of his love, not of an addiction to love. So here I was again, in the same boat as ten years before. Except that, with Matt, I was the innocent one and the relationship transformed me into an assertive and controlling woman. With Steve, I tapped into my dark side, a side I didn't know existed. I did things that I did not think I was capable of. I was a woman who'd abandoned her good morals. Now I understood that each of us has a good side and an evil side, and that we are capable of tapping into both. But we must choose integrity, goodness, and righteousness.

Meanwhile, I felt so alone. Most of my friends had married and were living their full lives. I was angry, too. I did not know it at the time, but that is why Steve and I were attracted to each other—it was out of loneliness and anger. We both needed love and affection, and we thought we'd been connected because we were meant to be together like soul mates

are. The truth was that we were missing something. Something very important: *self-love.* That's the mistake that most people make by thinking that their soul mate will somehow complete them. It is simply a romantic notion.

I realized that Steve was a selfish coward, and that he'd been playing the victim all along. He was unhappy yet did not want to step out of his comfort zone. I again researched affairs and gathered that ours was what is called a "split-self affair," which is a notch down from an "exit affair." Steve wanted to leave but was not ready because his children were still young. He refused to take responsibility for his actions, blaming others for his unhappiness. But in the end, playing the victim is self-defeating—it allows people to avoid standing up for themselves and makes building strength and confidence impossible. And it reinforces low self-esteem.

I am sure that our spiritual love was somehow karmic. We must have been lovers in a previous life who had met up in this one to continue the story and resolve remaining issues. Unfortunately, they were not resolved in this lifetime. I am positive that we will meet again in our next lifetime, under different circumstances, because there was so much love and understanding; because when we separated, we were still madly in love; and because one night, I heard his voice through transparent communication distinctly saying, "I would like to move forward in time to be with you." I believe his spirit knew he still needed time to grow, and when it did, he would be with me.

"I can't" is not in my vocabulary, nor should it be in yours. Always look for the positive side of things, because, truly, there are endless possibilities. Speaking from experience, I must say that an affair teaches a very hard lesson, and I would not recommend it. But if you take even the most difficult experiences as lessons, they will open your eyes and push you to grow.

◆ ◆ ◆

CHRISTINA'S THOUGHTS

❖ Make your home your haven. Your home should portray your personality, so spend time designing it to help you achieve a vision that speaks to your soul. Choose every piece of furniture very carefully. The result is a space that you'll *love* to live in.

❖ Buy yourself flowers from time to time. They will lift your spirit, especially in the wintertime.

❖ Always try to understand what happened and the reason why, because there is a lesson to be learned in everything that the universe throws at you.

❖ Go to bed early so that you'll get plenty of sleep and be able to wake up without the alarm. You will feel refreshed and ready for the day.

❖ Take time for yourself. Society tells us that if we do things for ourselves, then we must be selfish. NO! By taking care of ourselves, we recharge and are able to better take care of others. Go for a haircut periodically, and treat yourself to manicures and pedicures as often as you need them. When you do these things, it's not about the services as much as it's about how they make you feel. And you want to feel good, don't you?

❖ Listen to upbeat music. Latin music is fun, and it will automatically change your mood. If you need to unwind, classical, jazz, or opera are great. Put on some music and dance in your living room! This is an excellent way to release tension and to get in touch with your soul.

❖ Take time to evaluate your life. What are your priorities? What needs to change? What are you satisfied with? What are you not?

(A) I am whole
I am healed
I am Balanced
I am healthy

I want someone who is whole
→ I am whole now!

(B) I am love
If you want love
Be love!
I am love now

(C) I am vibrant.
I am I fun —
I have energy.
I am alive.
I am Radiant
I am my Spirit.
La gioie vivre].
organic Daughter

I am attractive
→ I am yummy
I am happy/smiley
↳ Be happy!] fun!
If you want someone happy/fun
↳ Be that
I am intune 2/3/12

(D) I am enlightened
→ If you want someone Spiritual/
↳ Be that Enlightened/Connected to God
I will be on 2/3/12

Reminders to always embrace my positive intentions.

CHAPTER 4

Integration

Timelessness
Such joy it brings
Peacefulness
Such divinity
A wind of love
Ravishes in vanity
Happiness
Many smiles in gravity
Fearlessness
Such awakening
Goodness
So rewarding . . .

My vacation was coming up and I was thinking about staying in New York. Though I love to travel around the world and to learn from different cultures, I did not have a specific place in mind to visit.

I believe intuition is very subtle and an amazing natural tool that can help us to guide our lives. One day, I was sitting on a bench in the park when *Santa Fe* popped in my head. After that, I started getting articles in the mail about Santa Fe. It was very strange. I'd never thought about going there before, and I believed that this was God's way of telling me to book a flight. A friend of mine told me that Santa Fe is a spiritual realm and home to a thriving artistic community.

My mother agreed to go with me. Neither of us had been to the desert lands of America before. We flew to Albuquerque, and from there we rented a car and drove for two hours to Santa Fe. It was during the month of October, the weather was beautiful, the sky was clear, and the temperature was perfect. There we experienced, for the first time, the adobe style of architecture—the terra-cotta houses and their colored windows made a big impression on my mother and me. We heard that many Native Americans still lived in the area, so we decided to visit an Indian reservation and hire a guide to explain their heritage to us.

I had another vacation three months later. Serendipity struck again when I heard about Sedona.

Apparently, this was another New Age mecca and artists' haven. I learned of the vortexes, which are mountains with electromagnetic fields that emanate healing energy. I did not understand their power; I definitely wanted to experience this land. My mother was curious as well. So we went.

Driving from Phoenix to Sedona, we saw large cacti for the first time in our lives. The scenery looked like the background of a Western movie. The first day, we took the tour of the vortexes, guided by a sweet-spoken lady wearing a lot of jewelry. She told us that there are lots of vortexes around the area, but four major ones are the most popular. Two of them, Airport Mesa and Boynton Canyon, emanate masculine energy, and the other two, Cathedral Rock and Bell Rock, emanate feminine healing energy. The Airport Mesa vortex was close to our hotel, so we spent most of our time there. From the top, we could see the most beautiful sunsets, and in the mornings I would wake up full of energy. Toward the end of the trip, we learned that whatever energy one brings to Sedona is amplified a million times.

I wanted to get my aura photographed. I had never done that before and was curious! The day before our departure, I found a woman who could *see* auras, so I made an appointment for the next day. But I wasn't totally happy about it because I was hoping to get a photograph as proof.

The following morning, we drove around a creek to find Indian Point, another beautiful spot with healing energy. My mother and I drove back and forth but couldn't find the secluded spot. I was starting to getting frustrated when my mother suggested that we go for a quick lunch and try again in the afternoon. The hotel had given us the name of a quaint little restaurant, but the directions were confusing. We drove around some more, finally spotting the restaurant on the other side of the road. We made a U-turn and found ourselves in a small parking lot in front of a small store. My mother looked up and said, "Look! Look!" On the store's window, written in big bold letters, was: PHOTO AURA HERE. I was very excited. We'd had to get lost in order to land right where we needed to be! I canceled the other appointment and my wish came true.

However, when I got my picture, I did not like what I saw. My aura was completely red. That signified anger—and lots of it! I thought I had healed, but I had not. The photographer suggested that I go to Indian Point. Was it coincidence? I do not think so. After lunch, we took the road to the creek, and this time we found the spot on the very first try!

We each sat down on a large stone in the middle of the creek. I meditated for a couple hours with tears rolling down my face, just like the river itself. That day I cried and cried, cleansing my past and preparing myself for a blissful future. I regret that I did not take a photo of my aura on the first day in Sedona. That way, I would have known which vortexes I needed to go to because, as it turned out, the ones I went to amplified my anger instead of healing it. So if you go to Sedona, which I absolutely encourage you to do, get your aura photo taken the first day.

I had read an article about crystals and their healing power, particularly the quartz crystal. So I went into a shop that had a big display of various kinds of crystals. I was attracted to one tucked way at the back of a shelf. The sun was hitting it just right, giving it a beautiful sparkle. I immediately purchased it. Once I got back to New York, I held it every night, feeling its healing energy bathe my heart and soul, the electric energy flowing like a current. I believe the crystal accelerated my healing process.

On a beautiful crisp autumn afternoon, I went for a walk in the woods near my house. I started crying, praying for God to help me. When I got back home, I held the crystal and asked for guidance. I suddenly got the urge to call Steve. Why, after so many months, I cannot tell you. When he heard my voice, he immediately said, "Where are you? Can I see you?" I had a feeling that I needed to help him.

We agreed to meet for lunch the next day. When I first saw him, he seemed withdrawn. He sat down with his arms crossed in front of his chest, as if guarding his heart, and leaned his body away from me. He was not the same man I had known. I told him that I was suffering from a broken heart. "You are not the only one," he said, sadness in his face. I could tell that he was suffering just as much as I was. I told him that I was willing to go to therapy with him, so that we could get to the bottom of his weakness—that's how much I loved this man. I would have done anything to be with him.

"I will think about it and will give you the answer by the end of the week," he replied.

"Are you still in love with me?" I asked.

"YES!" he said in a hopeful voice. "I can't help but love you!" The love was still there but the trust between us was lost. And that was a big issue.

Steve called me at the end of the week. Answering the phone, I felt happy because I thought there was still hope. Unfortunately, his voice was very cold, very distant and fearful. His reply was a straight NO. I gathered that Steve was under pressure and not able to make decisions, and that perhaps he was afraid. His last words to me, said with anger in his voice, were: "It's not that I do not want to, it's that I can't. You're the best thing that ever happened to me. Everything is perfect between us. Don't you think that I am angry that I cannot be with the woman I love? I am missing something and maybe you are, too. That's why I have decided to join a church and find Jesus."

"But I am the one who brought you closer to God, and now you are just going to throw me in the trash after all that?" I answered, angry as well. He was speechless. That was the last conversation we had. I've always wondered how two people who were once so close to each other, so madly in love, could become so angry and cold.

It saddens me when I see people who are miserable in their marriages and feel trapped in their lives. Some divorce; others sacrifice their happiness in order to stay for the kids like Steve did. If you decide to stay together, both partners should agree to seek spiritual growth; otherwise, if only one

person is trying to evolve, the other will always hold that partner back.

Once you are married and have children to tend to and food to get on the table, it is so much harder to work on yourself. I admire every married couple who has taken the spiritual path seriously and finds the time to meditate and go to yoga classes, because I know how hard it is. I feel fortunate that I was single during my spiritual growth because even though I went through painful breakups, I did not have responsibilities and, therefore, had a lot of time to concentrate on myself. Through my reading of many spiritual and self-help books, I learned how to cope with difficult situations and turn them around for my benefit.

One evening, I held the crystal in my hands, knelt on my knees, and, with tears in my eyes, prayed with all my heart for help from the divine. I wanted desperately to end the suffering, end the pain that was too much to bear. I wanted to stop thinking about Steve every second and to stop hoping and wondering whether he would ever come back into my life.

For the next couple months, I felt lost. I did not know what to do with my life. I had a job that was neither creative nor challenging. One day, I was talking to my friend Susan and, with desperation obvious in my voice, I asked her if she had any advice. She replied, "Yes, I do." I was curious about what she would say, since Susan was not into spirituality; she was more the logical type. However, her advice would alter my life completely and set me on the right track. She gave me the name of a life coach who happened to be her friend. What is a life coach? I had never heard of that. I researched it on the Internet and found it to be an interesting process.

I felt comfortable with life coach Linda from the get-go. We started off by concentrating on the types of jobs that I would be best suited for, but during our second session, the conversation switched to the topic of Miami, and the tone of my voice immediately shifted, reflecting how excited and happy I felt about the lifestyle of the city. Five years earlier, I'd gone to Miami on vacation. I felt so good that, after the first day, I'd called my mother to ask her to fax my résumé so I could apply for jobs at various hotels. I was hired right away and was very excited to go back to New York and pack my things. However, when I told my father about my plans, he gave me a whole speech about how my salary was not enough to survive on, and that I was going to be in debt within a couple months. His warnings instilled fear in me, so I dropped my plans to move. I told Linda that I'd always regretted that decision. But now, with my new furniture, it was harder to just pick up my suitcases and go, like I used to do. And I did not have the savings to move there. I came up with a whole bunch of excuses about why it would not be feasible, but in reality, it was only that same old fear.

After that session, I began to think more and more about the move. And one day, I woke up with a decision: I was going to quit my job and relocate to Miami and see what the future would hold for me there. Sheer excitement had replaced fear. God must've had a plan for me, and the year before surely had prepared me for the move to Miami. If you're ready to make changes in your life, and you're open to new ideas, I'd highly recommend hiring a life coach. Unlike more traditional forms of psychotherapy that deal with your past, life coaching deals with your future and helps you reach your highest potential. I'd also recommend Anthony Robbins's book *Awaken the Giant Within*, which I read between sessions and found to be very motivating.

One week before the move to Florida, I started feeling tingling on my forehead again. I had a massage appointment after work one evening—I had originally scheduled it for five thirty, but the masseuse had called to push it back to six o'clock because she was running late. So I decided to walk around the city during that extra time before the appointment, and I found myself near Steve's office. I looked at my watch and saw that it was five forty-five. Knowing that he got out at six, I was not worried about bumping into him. But the tingling was getting stronger, and suddenly I looked to the other side of the street, and there he was. My body started shaking as I tried to contain the anger boiling inside me, and I hid behind a car and waited for him to pass by. At that moment, I realized that I was not in love with him anymore. New York City has millions of people walking its streets night and day. What made me recognize Steve a block away and among the crowd remains a mystery to me.

When Steve had told me that he'd decided to find Jesus instead of being with me, I got angry at God. Why did God choose me to help Matt and

Steve become closer to him, yet I was the one to be left alone in the end? But now, as I reflect on what happened, I feel blessed because those two people helped me become whole, and I've become closer to God than I ever imagined I would be. The inner peace that comes from that integration is indescribable.

I am not a big fan of organized religion. I think it divides humanity, while spirituality embraces everyone and at the same time promotes individuality. I respect each person's different road to achieve growth. Now that I have a solid belief, my fear is gone, and I know that everything will be okay, that there is no need to worry. I don't watch television very often, but I used to watch a program called *It's a Miracle*. That show gave me a lot of hope and faith. It was about uncanny coincidences and how they change people's lives. There were many very touching stories that led me to truly believe in a bigger plan. When something wonderful happens in our lives, we believe in God. However, I have noticed that, for me, as soon as the event passes, I tend to forget about God. I finally understand that the key is to stay constant in faith through the good and the bad times, because ultimately everything is all good.

One day soon after that, I went into a store that sold home decorations. On the counter, next to the cashier, was a bowl full of stones with words engraved on them. I picked out four stones without looking at them. When I got back to my apartment, I was surprised when I read the words: LOVE FAITH GROWTH PEACE

It was exactly what my life was about at that moment. Isn't that an uncanny coincidence?

As my faith grew, I also began to become more aware of my thoughts. I could see that when I was being negative, things would not work out. On the mornings when I woke up thinking that the day was going to be a bad one, lo and behold, it would turn out either stressful, or a series of mishaps would occur. I used to say to myself that I'd been right after all. But in actuality, I had caused the day to be a bad one through my negative thinking. I am sure many of you can relate. Nowadays, every morning, I look up at the sky and say, "Good morning, God. Today is going to be a beautiful day." And you know what? It works. Starting your day with a positive thought orients your mind in a positive way. And even if bad things happen, you will be ready to greet them with patience and serenity, to let them pass without allowing them to affect your emotions. In New York City's subways, on the way to work, I used to observe the anxious people and their reaction to the usual stop-and-go routine of rush hour. Most people huffed and puffed and made faces, as if that was going to somehow alter the situation. Of course they were just wasting their energy. Meanwhile, the relaxed people just sat there, reading their papers or daydreaming, until they got to their stations. Those folks had the right idea.

I feel lucky that I did not have to battle any demons, that really I only got a taste of them. I did not have to overcome addiction—I needed to become whole. Now I feel more balanced. My emotions are more constant, and strong; unshakable trust and patience have become part of me.

Life is an experience, with cycles of highs and lows. It changes constantly. The only thing that is constant is *change*. I know many of you are scared of change. Please don't be. It's a wonderful process. You just have to go with it, because if you don't, your growth will stagnate. I know that staying in the comfort zone is the easy way, but try to step outside of it. I urge all of you to be courageous. The reward will be a fantastic life.

I truly believe that happiness comes from traveling the spiritual path and deeply studying your own soul. The more integrity and truth you develop, the closer to God you become, and the closer to God you become, the more you become in touch with love and compassion.

I have always admired my mother's unconditional love. I did not think I was capable of that kind of love until God brought two people into my life to test it. One of them was Steve. Our relationship opened our hearts, so much so that there wasn't room for anything else. I recall one day we had a fight, which was rare. When I apologized, he said, "I forgave you right away." When he said those words, I felt safe, that it was okay to be vulnerable, and, in that moment, I understood what it means to love unconditionally.

Yet, throughout our time together, I kept asking myself: Was my relationship with Steve about love or fear? I concluded that it was love based on fear, a love of codependency. As I moved toward wholeness,

I noticed that the love I feel has neither fear nor control nor selfishness, making it a win-win situation.

The other person who tested my unconditional love is a dear friend of mine. I was arguing with Cindy about her life choices—I wanted to transform her from a codependent person to an independent one, so that she could reach her highest potential. I wanted that happiness so much for her. But Cindy stuck to her decisions. In the past, if I disagreed with a friend about a big issue, I would not keep in touch with him or her, and basically I would give up the friendship. But with Cindy, I had another experience. Something pushed me to hold on to our relationship—I was learning to love unconditionally, to respect people's decisions, and to let them learn life's lessons in their own way. I then realized that I did not need to try to save people anymore, because I had saved myself.

All my life, I had been looking for my soul mate, when in actuality, what I was searching for was my own soul. I was dating someone when I realized that about myself. Later I asked him what he was most passionate about, and, his eyes wide, he replied, "I am most passionate about finding my soul mate." At that point I knew where he was in his life. Could I have explained to him, at that moment of truth, what I'd discovered about soul mates? I don't think so, because I believe the only way to grasp that idea is to live the experience.

Not everyone has the courage to change his or her life, and most people prefer to take the easy road. I believe that a lot of people would rather look for happiness outside of themselves, and that sometimes marriage is a way to escape the harder spiritual path. Yet a spiritual love connection can be a powerful catalyst for our growth. I believe there were two great romantic loves that came into my life to transform me. The first love transformed me from an innocent and naïve girl into an assertive and controlling woman. The second love transformed me from an assertive and controlling woman into a self-loving and integrated human being who has found, more than ever, faith in God. By taking responsibility for my choices and actions in life, I've become less selfish.

When you have the courage to look inside yourself, to really dig deep into your soul, you will find a treasure of happiness. But for that to happen, you will have to endure some difficult times. Unfortunately, God does not give us everything on a silver platter. Yet why live in misery, when all it takes is a little effort to create a joyful life?

◆ ◆ ◆

CHRISTINA'S THOUGHTS

❖   Do things you've wanted to do, feel things you've never felt before, and say things you've never said before. You will be proud.

❖   Make lunch the main meal of the day. Don't eat at night or, if you do, make it a light meal. You'll

feel better, sleep better; you'll even experience vivid dreams and intuition.

❖ When making a decision, be aware of how it makes you feel. If it lights you up, then it is the right decision. If, on the other hand, you feel confused, then it is the wrong one.

❖ If you drive to work, leave ten minutes earlier than you usually do so you can beat the traffic. These few minutes can make a big difference— you might even have time to do something you enjoy, like stop by a nearby café and read the newspaper, and you will arrive at the office more relaxed.

❖ Visualize your dream as if it is already a reality. Then start working out the details of how you will achieve that dream. In other words, work backwards.

❖ Have a massage once a month. It is a great way to release all the tension from the hard work you have been doing. You will feel like a new person, ready to tackle your life again. To me, it is like going to the doctor for a checkup, only much more fun!

❖ Take friendships very seriously. Invest in your friends, and you will create a wonderful connection.

CHAPTER 5

A Transitional Time

With Reem, Mom, and my brother, Khalil, at Club Med.

Overlooking the bay from the hotel balcony 5:45 a.m.
Softly, the awakening of another morning
Forever grateful for a view like this,
A moment ever so beautiful . . .
A morning so clear, so pure . . .
Waters so blue, so serene . . .
The sounds of birds . . .
A love dialogue in song . . .

Such hopeful greenery around
A magnificent sunrise over the bay
An indescribable peace and tranquility
Seeping into the inner depths of my soul . . .
Nothing ungodly about this very minute
And this very hour of the morning except the fact
    that I am parting with this setting in a few days.
Moments of plenty! Nevertheless . . .
Taking the memory of it all with me is a blessing
    my innermost self cannot deny . . .
The shimmering waters salute a towering tree
    above . . .
They both assure each other's presence . . .
Reminding the viewer that distance is no problem!
Love and lovers prevail over all and everything.
The totality of those surroundings.
What a breathtaking thrilling sensual experience!
A small boat leaving the marina seems to cross the
    waters to eternity . . .
God! It is such a magnificent moment
All I ask is to live such moments as often as possible
Only to have more strength
To show my gratitude through what I can do and
    give to others . . .
My ecstasy at this moment is beyond words . . .
Beyond description . . . I am totally overwhelmed.
Engulfed by the transparency of all this beauty
    around!
Suddenly the horizon is within reach . . .
Within touch!
A most exhilarating experience unsheathes and
    unravels uncertainties.

Only to discard them as irrelevant . . .
At the mercy of all this translucent beauty
And the awe of its infinity . . . my very existence . . .
. . . to be continued on a next journey

When I arrived in Miami in 2004, my emotions were running high. I could not believe it: finally, after twelve years, I'd made it! I had no appetite whatsoever, and I'm sure my excitement was obvious from miles away. It was as if I was in love with the whole world!

At first, life in Miami was amazing. The city was so different from New York, where buildings are brown and the sky is gray, and Central Park is the only green spot. In Miami, the pastel-painted buildings and Mediterranean-style houses reminded me of Spain and the South of France, and the Latin cultural influence gave the whole city a feeling of joy and freedom. I cannot tell you how much the bright colors lifted my spirit every day. The smell . . . Ah! That tropical freshness and ocean breeze compelled me to expand my lungs and breathe in as much air as I could. That's what I did every day: really breathe. I took a yoga class on the beach—an amazing experience—and felt my senses heightening. I felt expansive and, for the first time, optimistic about creating a purposeful life.

So inspired, I became very focused and devoted to defining my purpose. I wanted stability and a job that I would look forward to every morning. As soon as I read Dr. Wayne Dyer's *The Power of Intention* and grasped the concept, I started applying it and discovered it was very helpful in attracting what I desired. And once I'd settled in to my new home, I looked for a place that took aura photos, because I was curious to see the changes that had occurred in me.

I had read about the chakras in various books, but to actually see a picture of them was a different story. For further information, consult the excellent book *Wheels of Life,* by Anodea Judith.

The aura camera has got to be the best invention for spiritual growth. With the photograph, I was to receive a reading of my chakras from Mathilda, a genuine and helpful woman in a bright blue shirt, black pants, and high heels, her long hair pulled back into a ponytail, emphasizing the pleasant shape of her face. But before I went into Mathilda's studio, something very strange happened. Hearing that I might need to write some notes, I looked around for a blank piece of paper and found a typed paper on the counter by the cash register. I didn't even glance at it, just folded it up and brought it in with me, thinking that I could use the blank side for my notes. Mathilda advised me on what to do in order to open my chakras and become more balanced, and I was amazed at how accurate and informative her reading was. It would become the compass for my purpose. When we were finished, she asked me if the paper was mine. I said to her that it was for my notes, but since I did not actually write anything on it, she could throw it away. She unfolded it and said, "Did you read what is typed here? It is exactly what

you need right now. You should call this woman for an appointment. It will do you a lot of good."

I was baffled. This paper that I'd nearly thrown out turned out to be crucial for my healing! Written on it was a brief description of "transformational breathing," and the name and telephone number of the lady who facilitated it. I had never heard of this kind of breathing before. Of course, my curiosity led me to research it further on the Internet. We are so lucky to have the Internet. It is amazing how much information we can access, on any and every subject that we could ever think of. I was intrigued by what I found. I made an appointment right then—since I knew I would benefit from it, why not jump right in? After all, I am all for growth.

Maya, a short woman with a sweet face and lovely brown eyes, wore a sleeveless print dress and a turban on her head. She explained the process to me, which seemed easy because you just lie on the floor and breathe. Yes, that was it! But the key was to breathe without pause between breaths for forty-five minutes straight. This brings a large quantity of oxygen into the brain, allowing the human being to access higher consciousness.

It was an interesting session. I cried at times, and I found it hard to focus on my breath for such a long time, especially because it was stirring up my emotions. So it turned out not to be so easy after all! Maya suggested that I come back for a session of ERT, or Emotional Release Therapy. What's that, you ask? It's another spiritual process that I had not heard of. I agreed to do it the following week. In the meantime, I went back to New York City for a few days. There, I saw a friend who gave me a book called *The Mastery of Love* by Don Miguel Ruiz. I read most of it once I got back to Miami. Right before the ERT session, I ran out of time and, preferring not to rush, I left the last two pages to finish later.

From my Internet research, I had a vague idea of what to expect, but to experience it was something else. The room had four small windows to let the sun shine through, and on the yellow walls were a few Asian decorative pieces. Maya asked me to lie down on the massage table. With a big smile on my face, I lay down, thinking it was going to be relaxing like the massages I get once a month. I was *ready*. Then, all of a sudden, I felt Maya's hand squeezing the muscles of my back. AY!!! That was the beginning of an hour and a half of pure torture. I cried from the pain, which was physical mixed with emotional. Of course, Maya had a box of tissues handy, and at one point I felt like I was crying from the very depth of my soul. It was the best process I have ever experienced. It allowed me to release so much suffering, and I got a clearer understanding of my low self-esteem, which had always been powered by the idea that I was not intelligent. That session helped me to replace the bad seed of "not good enough" with "self-love," "understanding," and "peace." Afterward, I resumed my reading of *The Mastery of Love* and was very surprised to see that the last two pages were about self-love, solidifying my understanding of what had happened in the ERT session. If I had read those pages before, they would not have impacted me as much.

The next day, I decided to go for an early afternoon walk. I'd put on my tennis shoes and was headed for the door when all of a sudden my throat started to hurt. It felt as if someone were choking me. I sat down and tried to calm down. My intuition told me that I needed to squeeze something out of my soul, so I took out my notebook and started writing. I found myself forgiving everyone who had ever hurt me in the past as a river of tears flowed down my cheeks and onto the table. I wrote about ten pages on understanding and forgiveness. Afterward, I looked in the mirror and saw that my eyes were all puffy and red but my face seemed serene. I had released all the pain and suddenly looked much younger. It was an odd incident, but I am glad it happened.

A few weeks after the ERT session, I went in for another breathing session. This time, I had a completely different experience. My breathing became deeper and flowed quite easily. I smiled the whole time and left the session with a sense of peacefulness and radiance. I was so happy to feel that way that I assigned myself forty-five minutes of breathing at home every day. Because of this exercise, the tingling I'd felt on my forehead—the connection from my spirit to Steve's spirit—was replaced with a strong intuition, which became the connection to my own spirit.

I went back to Mathilda for a follow-up of the aura photography session. She was amazed at the changes. "It shows that you are doing a lot of work," she said with a smile. I found out that I had an orange aura, which meant that I was a creative person. All this time I knew I was creative, yet I was choosing jobs that were more administrative and, therefore, killing my spirit. Mathilda also introduced me to crystals that balance the chakras. I'd worked with the healing quartz crystal before, but the concept of a specific crystal for each chakra was new to me. I decided to buy all seven of them and added the fifteen-minute crystal ritual to my breathing routine. As you can see, it takes a lot of time to do it all, but I was dedicated to my growth. After that, I started waking up with lots of energy, so I began to take long walks on the beach. One morning, I was feeling particularly good when I looked up at the sky and felt myself becoming one with the birds. I sat down in front of the sea and literally felt the motion of the waves. My body was swaying! It was such a peaceful experience. Tears rolled down my cheeks. "Life is beautiful!" I screamed.

During the aura reading, Mathilda had told me that my spirit guide was nearby and that he would reveal himself in a very creative way. A couple days later, I got an intuition to go to the botanical gardens. I drove there the next day, and, walking around the grounds, I looked for a sign that would show me who my spirit guide was. I was disappointed that day, and after one month went by and there was still no sign, I felt resigned that I would never meet him, and I let it go. Yet one night a little bit after that, I was sleeping when I smelled trash. I was in my own bedroom and knew there was no trash there, because

I always emptied the can. When I woke up the next morning, I had a burst of energy. I changed my bedroom completely, arranging two colorful sheets to create a beautiful space around my desk. I had a strange feeling, as though I was not the one coming up with these creative ideas. Then I remembered the smell. When I put two and two together, I concluded that the smell was actually my spirit guide revealing himself in a very creative way. I also remembered that same smell from eight years earlier, when he came to comfort me in a time of despair. I don't know why my spirit guide smells bad, but I am grateful for his help during these transformations.

Six weeks after the photo was taken, I took another one. I was amazed at the colorations. Through ERT, I had completely healed my heart, and the crystals had opened up my previously closed chakras.

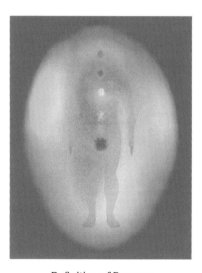

Definition of Purpose

I had a lot of energy that was being wasted in the first chakra that needed to move upward to the seventh chakra, which is consciousness. Notice that the red circle is large, which meant that my root chakra was overactive. Mathilda informed me that when that energy moved up, I would be able to define my purpose in life. She suggested that I take Kundalini yoga classes. Kundalini is not as popular as hatha yoga; however, it is a very powerful type of yoga, and it has a particular way of working with the breath. During a relaxation in Kundalini yoga class, I felt a surge of energy go up my spine and saw an image of a dove flying from my heart. It was a beautiful moment. The dove, the symbol of peace, signified that my heart was healing.

I wanted to be inspired, because the word "inspire" means "to guide by divine inspiration." I also wanted to find something that had meaning to me, that I was qualified to do, and with which I would contribute to the world. I did not want to work just for a paycheck anymore. And that's the way everybody should feel. If we want the world to become a better place, we each have to contribute our own unique talents.

The Kundalini yoga helped me a lot, and my next aura photograph proved that.

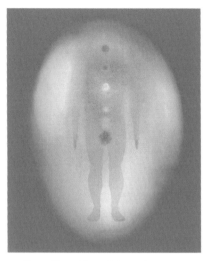

Transformation of Consciousness

Mathilda gave me a clue about my purpose. She said it consisted of: creativity, communication, and spirituality. Those were the three nouns for me to start with. I knew I was onto something big, and I was feeling more relaxed and excited about the idea. What could it possibly be? At first, the three nouns did not make sense to me. One morning, I was watching television and saw Stephen Covey talking about his new book, *The 8th Habit*. I got curious about the book and bought it, and I was happy to find that it was exactly what I needed. In one of the chapters, he wrote about finding our own true voices. Yes . . . that was what I needed to find! I was astonished that I had been led to my next step by coincidentally pausing on a TV channel. I really felt that it was the right time for me, since I was aware of who I was as a person, and the universe was somehow pushing me toward defining my purpose. Covey also mentioned that we should move to the city or town where we feel most comfortable and happy. And that's exactly what I'd done when I moved to Miami. I also purchased Richard N. Bolles's *How to Find Your Mission in Life* and *What Color Is Your Parachute?* and *The Path: Creating Your Mission Statement for Work and for Life*, by Laurie Beth Jones.

I got so excited from reading these books and doing the exercises they suggested. One of those exercises involved choosing words that were attractive to me from a list, and grouping them by similarity. The results fell into three categories, which immediately revealed to me what my purpose consisted of:

Advance	Communicate	Write
Brighten	Connect	Create
Motivate	Speak	Creativity
Inspire	Share	
Encourage	Educate	
Enlighten	Communication	
Affect		
Enthuse		
Heal		
Integrate		
Illuminate		
Spirituality		

It frustrates me to see that people choose to stay miserable and stagnant in their lives, and it excites me to see people grow and take the spiritual path. I could help them grow and reach their highest potential. I wanted to communicate, inspire, and enlighten,

bringing joy to human development and spirituality. From that insight, I wrote my mission statement:

"My mission is to help angry and miserable people grow closer to God, to find their souls, and to reach their highest potential living a life of purpose."

I believe that everyone should have a mission statement, which represents his or her purpose in life. Soon after that, I went in to have another aura photo taken.

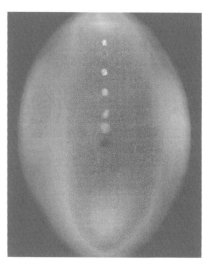

Manifestation

Notice the white circle on the top of my head, corresponding to my seventh chakra. It appeared for the first time because I'd connected with my higher consciousness.

I had not been very interested in reading until I found the subject of spirituality. From then on, I was hooked on books. I love books. They have helped me through this journey, and I would absolutely love to be an inspiration for the growth of all humanity.

When you define your purpose in life, you will connect with the divinity within you. That's when happiness becomes part of your daily life. That's when your life is complete, when your spirit flows like creeks, rivers, and oceans. There will be no clouds floating in the sky of your soul. When I think back on my own journey, I realize that I have spent half my life searching and the other half living in alignment with the universe.

After those first five months of exploration and trying to get my life together in Miami, I began thinking about how great it would be to get a job with responsibility in a creative industry. I wanted to experiment with graphic design, and just as I was pondering the idea of signing up for classes on Adobe Photoshop and Illustrator, I got a job as an art coordinator, overseeing ten graphic designers. It was unbelievable. So I got to learn about the programs while being paid. It was great!

It is true that more often than not, our thoughts attract what we desire. "Be careful what you wish for" is a saying that I've heard a million times, as I am sure you have as well. But I never believed it until I started to notice that whenever I thought of something, it happened. So I finally understood the reality of that saying.

All this time, whenever I passed by the locals' favorite Starbucks, the same man smiled at me and cordially said hello. Not willing to let anyone near my heart again, I'd always return his smile and then hurry off to work.

One Saturday afternoon, the universe had a mysterious plan for me. After my painting class, I was walking home, my hands and face streaked with paint, when I heard someone say, "Hello!" I was feeling insecure about my disheveled appearance so I just kept walking. But after a few steps I felt as though a force was turning me around and pushing me like a puppet toward the man who'd said hello. It was so strong that when I stopped, I nearly fell over. It was one of the strangest supernatural events I have experienced—and a wonderful divine intervention.

Here was the same man who had been smiling at me for the past five months. I'd never really looked closely at him before—he was a tall, well-built man with soft black eyes, in khaki pants and a navy-blue shirt. I had no choice but to finally introduce myself, and he told me that his name was Michael. He gave me his card and said, "Give me a call soon, okay?" I nodded yes, but in my head I was really thinking that I wouldn't!

A week passed and, by a twist of fate, I ran into him again. "You did not call me," he said with a surprised look on his face. Then he asked for my number. Since I'd had a whole week to think about him and had come to the conclusion that he seemed like a nice man, I was no longer hesitant and was happy to give him my number.

The next morning, while I was walking on the beach, my phone rang. "Hello, this is Michael calling. What are you doing at the moment?" he said with a hint of shyness in his voice.

"I am walking on the beach and taking pictures," I answered cheerfully.

"Do you mind if I join you?" he said.

"No, not at all," I replied.

Michael and I ended up talking until the late hours of the night. We realized that we had a lot in common, that we both had gone through some painful experiences but had found the strength to survive. It was great to meet a kindred soul. Soon we were inseparable.

One day, during one of my oil-painting classes, I'd been deep in concentration when I turned to my left to look for the red cadmium paint. Michael was standing there. "How long have you been here?" I asked, shocked. "I have been standing here for a while now," he answered with a big smile. We both started laughing.

Michael soon moved in with me. I knew that I was ready to experience what it was like to live with someone and to share a life. He became a catalyst for my spiritual growth. He loved to cook, and all day long I looked forward to our dinners, to the wonderful conversation and the music playing softly in the background. I also loved to cuddle with him on the living room sofa, watching television or a DVD that we had rented. I was experiencing something very different than I had in my previous relationships.

Michael brought me stability, companionship, friendship, and affection. A simple life. But I couldn't shake the feeling that something was missing . . . passion. I often asked myself, "Is it better to have passion, excitement, even craziness in one's life, or is it better to have the security of a stable relationship?" I missed that passion, but at the same time I loved the stability.

One day, while walking down Lincoln Road, I stopped at the symphony building and asked for a piano teacher. I'd always wanted to learn to play the piano, but I thought that I would wait until retirement to pursue it. Somehow, that day, I was inspired to try it, and I am glad I did. Playing the piano is very therapeutic and healing. It helps me to focus, and sometimes I find myself in meditation while playing the keys. I read somewhere that taking up a musical instrument later on in life is conducive to spiritual growth.

After a year, I realized that Miami was not the paradise I'd imagined it to be at all. It is a great place for a vacation, but actually living there is different—in short, I was bored. The job opportunities were scarce; it was hard to meet people outside of the nightclub scene; and there wasn't much to do. I was disappointed. For twelve years I'd wanted to settle there, and it had let me down. I did not know what to do. I felt frustrated—I just hadn't made enough progress, and I felt like I'd gotten on the wrong path. But I loved and still love the beauty of Miami: the bright colors, the palm trees, the turquoise-colored ocean, the smell of the tropical air—I miss those. And yet I realized I needed a change.

On February 1, 2006—two days shy of my fortieth birthday—something happened that would change my life forever. I *surrendered*.

"To surrender is one of the most comforting and pleasurable experiences available to humans. We are freed from the chains of our minds, we join the cosmic flow. We are happy, as we experience the embrace of the universal love."—Guru Rattana

I had tried to surrender a couple times before but found myself still with expectations and their resulting disappointments. This time it was different. I'd tried so hard to make things happen for me in Miami and had reached the point where I just gave up. I could not fight the universe anymore. I understood that it was not my will but God's plan for me, and so I let go of my dream of living in Miami.

Unsure of what to do next, I decided to go to New York City for a couple weeks. It was springtime. The weather was perfect, and flowers were blooming in Central Park. People were out, enjoying the weather after the long, cold winter. I'd missed the crowds and the culture of the city. I realized that, because I'd lived in big cities all my life, I could not live in a small village like Miami. It's true what they say about New York City: there is no place like it in the world. And so I decided to move back.

Upon my return to Miami, I broke the news to Michael. He was not very happy about it. Nevertheless, we cared about one another and each wanted the best for the other, so we parted on good terms. Our last day together, we hugged for a long time, aware of the bittersweet ending of our relationship.

Meanwhile, I was still giving a lot of thought to my purpose. As a humanitarian, I wanted to work for nonprofit organizations. However, I had to support myself, and I didn't know if I could do something I cared about that would also pay the bills. My friend Nicolas recommended *Secrets of the Millionaire Mind*, by T. Harv Eker. When I read the book, I was astonished to find out that a lot of our negative statements about money are ingrained in us since childhood, and that our own habits come from our parents' modeling of how to deal with money. For me, some of the negative statements were "Rich people are greedy" and "Money is not important," among others. Granted, I grew up in a wealthy environment, my family did not have financial problems, and my friends all wore designer clothing. But still, I had the idea that rich people are superficial and, as far as I can remember, I valued a simplicity of spirit that did not prioritize keeping up with the Joneses. Life for me had a deeper meaning than acquiring the newest Chanel bag. I preferred reading philosophy books and wondering about the universe and how I got here.

At the end of the book, the author invites the reader to a free three-day seminar, which I immediately signed up for. It was scheduled for June, just a few weeks before my move back to New York. It was the best thing that ever happened to me. I would recommend this seminar to anyone interested in finding financial freedom.

There were about eighteen hundred of us. We went through a lot of mental exercises, and the days were long but very informative. In one particular exercise, the speaker told us to read all the negative statements we had about money and then to visualize the statements going down a stream into a river and finally floating away. In the next exercise, he told us to write down positive statements and to read them. Well, I have to tell you, that was a very strange experience, because the first time I read the positive statements, my brain did not register them. I felt confused, and I did not really believe what I was reading. About half an hour later, I read them again and this time my brain accepted every single positive statement. Thus, my paradigm about money had shifted.

We had another experiment, in which someone sprinkled pennies on the floor and we had to look for them and keep one. My mother always seemed to find pennies wherever she went, while I, on the other hand, never bothered to look. On the rare occasion that I did see one, I would simply dismiss it. Now, for the first time in my life, I looked at a penny as though it were a diamond. It was no longer nil. That penny represented my acceptance of money. I *loved* that penny. I put it close to my heart, caressed it, and continued to kiss it every few minutes. Soon after the seminar, I started to find pennies everywhere, and every time, I would embrace them. My energy field had changed, and I'd become a money magnet.

I have to mention one more exercise from that seminar that was very revealing. We were divided into four groups based on how we'd filled out a questionnaire. The first group was the "Spenders." Spenders spend, and in essence they keep the economy running. I was stunned to see that they were 85 percent of the whole group.

The second group was the "Savers." Savers save but don't have much fun in life. They were 10 percent of the whole group.

The third group was the "Avoiders." They were 4 percent of the whole group. Amazingly, Avoiders do not open their bills!

And the fourth group was the "Monks." This is the group in which I found myself. We were 1 percent of the entire group.

Looking around the large conference hall, I wondered how and why I was included in this group and not the others. Through a lengthy discussion, I found out that our group's challenge was understanding that money has an energy of its own, and that money can be used for the greater good. We are humanitarians with the mission of making a difference. So if we create our wealth, we will not use it for the benefit of our egos but for helping others in need. And that's how I came to appreciate money and to no longer think of it as the root of all evil. Yes, money can be used in a healthy way!

On the second day of the seminar, I sat next to a woman who was about the same age as I was. Right away, I began to cry from the depth of my soul, and I opened up to her. I realized that I was irresponsible

with money and, at the age of forty, I was still searching for my purpose in life and still dependent on
my mother for financial help. Feelings of guilt and
shame overwhelmed me. I shook my head in disgust
and said, "I should be taking care of my mother at
this point. I am not a kid anymore." I was incredibly
angry at myself.

It's true what they say about anger: it's a great
motivator! From that day on, I vowed that I would
make a lot of money, that I would create a purpose
in life, that I would take care of my mother, even
spoil her as she had spoiled me. I was a changed
human being. The guilt and anger were replaced
by motivation and creativity, and later the shame
would be replaced by pride. The seminar gave me
confidence and got me over the fear of creating my
purpose.

When I got back from the seminar, I began to
prepare for the move in earnest. Right away I started
to have a hard time letting go of my furniture. I'd
handpicked every single piece, and everything was
meaningful to me. My furniture had become a part
of my identity, and I saw just how easy it is to get
attached to material things. A couple weeks before
I moved, I had a breakthrough about the furniture
and my belongings. As I looked around my apartment, I understood that by letting go of what I had, I
was letting go of my childhood, my identity as I knew
it, the little girl in me. Somehow I felt a transformation coming and realized that I was maturing, and I
was happy to sell everything because I was no longer
that person.

My last day in Miami was peaceful. I smiled as I looked around the apartment, thinking about the good times I'd had there. And I was looking forward to a fresh start in New York City.

◆ ◆ ◆

CHRISTINA'S THOUGHTS

❖ Read self-help and spiritual books—lots and lots of them! The information that you receive from them will be crucial to your growth.

❖ Organize your home and office, because a messy environment leads to confusion in your mind. If you are not an organized person, ask a friend or a neighbor to help you, or hire a professional organizer. It could be a lot of fun and I am sure you will gain a lot of space. You can also get ideas from the television shows that decorate and organize homes.

❖ Buy the stones and crystals that correspond to each chakra. Lie down on the floor and place garnet in between your thighs, tangerine quartz on your navel, citrine on your stomach, emerald on your heart, lapis on your throat, azurite on the third eye, and amethyst on the floor close to the top of your head.

❖ You have a unique talent. When you find it and use it, you delight others and yourself.

❖ Communicate with your significant other. It will help you become friends. Just remember, we are all vulnerable. When your guard is down and you speak from a place of authenticity, you'll experience a deeper connection. You will learn a lot about each other and most often you will find out that you share the same fears.

❖ The world is always a mirror image of you:
   ♦ When you smile at someone, you get a smile back.
   ♦ When you give love, you receive love.
   ♦ When you give money, you will get money in return.

❖ Be passionate about life. If you truly take the time to find your passion, you will live a wonderful and fulfilled life. It's true. Living from purpose is what God wants us to do.

CHAPTER 6

Creation of a Purpose and Success

Fragile . . . Why am I?
I would have liked to be strong
To be able to stand on Earth
A world as cruel as ours
Why do we live in these conditions?
Nobody's happy
Bad luck has always a way
Of scratching the human being
Leaving its traces for life
I think that freedom
Is the only joy that's left for us?
Only . . . Aren't we victims of an imprisonment of
    society?
Life leads us into narrow roads
It's up to us to be able to go through them
Even if sometimes with difficulty . . .

My circle of guidance.

In July, I moved back to New York, where I rejoiced in going to the theater, museums, and art galleries. I walked down the streets, taking in everything with fresh eyes, and I found myself falling in love with New York City all over again.

During the few weeks that followed, I picked up every beginner's book on finance that I could find. I went to my bank and proceeded to put my IRA account into a mutual fund. You see, on my twentieth birthday, my father had opened a trust fund for me. Which was great, except that he did not educate me on how to preserve and grow that fund. So, being young and foolish, I spent most of it and put the rest in a money market account, which had sat there without accruing any interest for twenty years.

After the seminar, I was very angry at my father for not showing me what to do with that money. Then I understood that, at the time, he did not know better. Many times we blame our parents for things that hurt us, but we must recognize that it is not always their fault. So I stopped blaming him and took it upon myself to get educated. My financial adviser purchased a good mutual fund, but after going to a couple of seminars on stocks, I realized that he was getting a hefty commission out of it. I was furious.

I was so angry at myself for being taken for a fool that I vowed to seize control of my finances. After all, who cares about my finances but me? Financial advisers want us to think that trading stocks is complicated, but in reality, it is very simple and it does not take a lot of time. I became obsessed, unstoppable in my attempt to absorb everything there was to know about the stock market.

When I felt confident enough to trade on my own, I went to my financial adviser and asked him to sell the mutual fund. "Why?" he asked. "This is a very good fund."

"Well, I lost one hundred dollars in the past month."

He looked at me and said, "Oh please!"

"It's a bullish market right now and, if this was a good fund, I should not have lost even one penny," I said. His face turned bright red.

"I see . . . you are knowledgeable about the stock market, then."

"Yes, indeed. I will be trading online on my own from now on."

"Good luck," he said, wide-eyed and probably thinking to himself that I was making a big mistake, and that I would lose all my money. I am happy to report that, since opening my online trading account, my stock portfolio has done very well and I have not lost a dime on my principal.

Anyone can trade stocks. The key is knowledge. Learn all you can about the companies you are interested in purchasing. Don't go into it blindly. Whenever you can, and I know that you are capable of it, save and invest in your future.

I was also interested in things beyond stocks. I'd met Janet during my first month back in New York City. She was a tall, slender woman with beautiful curly red hair. At our first meeting she wore casual pants with a colorful blouse and striking turquoise jewelry. She informed me that she was a shamanic healer and, curious, I scheduled an appointment with her. It turned out to be a very different kind of healing session than the ones I had experienced before.

Janet explained to me that she goes on a spiritual journey to find the parts of the soul that are missing.

"I'm sorry, but I do not understand what that means exactly. Janet, can you explain?" I asked.

"Our soul becomes fragmented through traumas and negative events in our lives," she said. "As children, our souls are intact, but through the years they are deprived of their wholeness. Happiness goes away; we feel the pain of losing a loved one; we hurt our bodies; addictions take hold of us; and we feel that we've lost part of our spirit. So I delve into the subconscious to find those missing parts and return them to your soul so that you become healed and whole again."

I understood the concept a bit better, but it was still not fully clear. And I was skeptical at first. After the journey, Janet told me that she had found two lost soul parts and restored them. Those parts were vitality and passion. At first, I did not think anything of it. But about a couple days later, a surge of energy and passion came upon me. I wanted to take dance classes! I put two and two together, and it became apparent to me that the healing session was the reason for how I was feeling. So I became a believer.

A month later, I returned for another session. Sometimes in shamanic journeys, animals reveal themselves as guides or totems, and for me, a fun-loving monkey appeared. He was water-skiing. This time, Janet found two other soul parts: fun and lightheartedness.

After the session, I was eager to see what was going to happen. Sure enough, a week later, I found myself Rollerblading in Central Park with my iPod blasting. I even took up horseback riding! I started reminiscing about my youth, remembering how my father used to say: "My little girl is a happy-go-lucky character. She is carefree and fun-loving; good for her." Unfortunately, like so many of us, I'd become more worried and serious, burdened with responsibility. So I was glad to see those parts back in my soul. After all, life without fun is pretty sad.

Janet also introduced me to flower essences, which can help our growth on a spiritual level. I went to a lecture at a yoga center to see what it was all about. The lecturer had a basket of cards, each with a different flower or plant painted on it. She asked me to pick one card. Sensing that I was a bit nervous, she laughed and said, "Don't be scared; whatever card you pick will be meant for you now." So I closed my eyes and picked the lily card. "This card means that the lily essence will help open up your feminine chakra. Take this bottle of essence, dilute the liquid with some water, and drink a little bit every morning. You will soon see change."

So I bought the little bottle of lily essence. Believe it or not, after I started using it, I began to feel more feminine. I had been wearing only pants for the past ten years, and all of a sudden I wanted to buy skirts! In the past, I only had natural color on my nails, and now I wanted to put on red nail polish. I even bought red lipstick. It was very strange. I was feeling sexy in the same way I had when I was in my twenties.

I concluded that, in my twenties, I had more yin (feminine traits), and then in my thirties, after my breakups with Matt and Steve, I became angry and assertive, taking on more yang (masculine traits). When I hit forty—and took this flower essence—I got back the feminine traits that I had lost. The yin/yang became more balanced as I grew closer to wholeness.

One day, I remembered something Michael had asked me: "Why aren't you with a successful man?" At that time, I did not know the answer. However, that question stayed in my head. *Why aren't I with a successful man?* I wondered.

A month later, I was reading an amazing book called *Are You the One for Me?* by Barbara De Angelis. A real eye opener! I found my answer in the book.

We tend to attract mirror images of ourselves, and since I was not successful in my own life and vibrated at a lower frequency, I attracted equally unsuccessful men. The book also revealed to me that my role in relationships tended to be "the rescuer." So, with that in mind, I declared that I was done rescuing men—I was going to rescue myself.

Meanwhile, I continued to read finance books, and I came to understand that I no longer wanted to be just an employee, and that the key to becoming wealthy is to have a lucrative business of your own. So I decided to become an entrepreneur.

If you want security in your life, then a salaried job is for you. Going out on your own takes courage, but I believe that each one of us has a unique purpose in life. Therefore I would say to you:

* Find a need
* Use your talent
* Leave a legacy

In September, after securing my stock portfolio, I began to work on building my preschool business. I am notorious for doing a spring-cleaning every year to keep my apartment empty of clutter, and this time, much to my surprise, I found all my files from my teaching days, intact. I could not believe that I had not thrown them out after so many years! This must have been the reason why. The files gave me a lot of helpful information for starting the process. Suddenly, everything began to fit together like pieces in a jigsaw puzzle.

My favorite professional years were those spent teaching.

I loved the Montessori philosophy and the independence the program gives children.

My preferred language is French.

During the Landmark Forum seminar, I'd created my mission: to unite children from various cultures.

All of this prepared me for my purpose. It was amazing.

When you look back at your life, you will recognize the sequence of events that led you to where you are at the present. The people you met along the way, the places you traveled to, the education you had, and the relationships you formed: all of it somehow comes together when you are living in alignment with your purpose. It is truly magical. And if you are analytical as I am, you will enjoy the

process of gathering the pieces and putting together the puzzle of what your life has become. Below is an example of a writing exercise for just that, so that you can create a job that uses your strength and aligns with your values. I've included my answers, but you can use the headings—assets, strengths, values, passions, and core needs—to find yours:

ASSETS:
    Positive thinker
    Smile

STRENGTHS:
    Organizer
    Planner
    Analytical
    Teacher
    Communicator
    Researcher
    Working with children

VALUES:
    Honesty
    Creativity
    Personal growth/learning
    Service/contribution
    Vitality
    Security
    Commitment
    Fun/humor
    Stability

PASSIONS:
    Creativity
    Children

CORE NEEDS:
    Nurturing children
    Financial security

Then, find the most important ones. These were mine:

    Creativity
    Fun/humor
    Working with children
    Teaching
    Service/contribution

And that's how I came up with the concept of Le Petit Paradis Preschool.

The preschool's mission was to create a harmonious international environment, unite children from different cultural backgrounds, and work in a team environment and a relaxed and positive atmosphere. It would give children an opportunity to learn French as a second language from a young age. By combining both Montessori and Bank Street philosophies, the children would receive an early start to a strong education. The school would contribute a unique service using education, psychology, communication, caring, and nurturing with elements of creativity, play, recreation, enthusiasm, fun, humor, and lots of love, resulting in confidence, independence,

high self-esteem, and overall happiness! That's why it is called The Little Paradise!

During the creation of the preschool, I felt a transformation occurring. I was maturing, becoming responsible and wise. I became *a woman*. I also mustered the courage to have varicose-vein surgery. My left leg had begun to hurt me to the point where I could walk for no more than half an hour at a time. So it was crucial that I went through the sclerotherapy treatments. I read that, in spiritual terms, varicose veins meant that the energy of life was not flowing through my body. And since my spirit was all about *la joie de vivre*, this was another reason to get rid of the blocked veins. I felt much better after the surgery.

The idea of the preschool filled my soul with such enthusiasm that, for the next couple months, I worked from sunrise to sunset. It was the first time in my life that I felt motivated, and since I am a very organized person, I truly loved being self-employed. I found myself on a roll, with everything coming together effortlessly. I knew exactly what to do, and when I ran into an obstacle, there was always something or someone that helped me to overcome it.

First, I researched the various types of corporations and opted for a C corporation, which was the best type for tax purposes. An acquaintance told me about a website for legal matters called www.legalzoom.com, which had the required forms to fill out. So instead of paying a lawyer to do all the paperwork, I did it myself, and along the way learned a lot about taxes. I'd advise anyone who is thinking of beginning a small business venture to do as much as possible on your own—that way you get to be involved from start to finish, and you will become more knowledgeable.

Next, I wanted to create a visual of what the space would look like. I asked my friend, who is an architect, to help me. It turned out beautifully. When the time came to create a website, I met with a graphic designer, but I was not satisfied with the designs he showed me. I mentioned my frustration to my brother, Khalil, and he suggested that I do it myself and gave me the name of a website—www .freewebs.com—that helps people create their own websites using their own concepts. Building my own site from scratch was a real treat. When I was done, I emailed the link to a couple of my friends for some honest feedback, and, much to my surprise, overall I did well. It just needed a few tweaks here and there, and then it was set to go. Of course, I could not post the website until the preschool was open.

Next, I researched educational materials, toys, books, and furniture for the classroom. Everything I needed, I found on the Internet. It was amazing; I did not need to leave my house. I made a list of everything I planned to order. With most of the administrative work done, I started to look for spaces. Soon I found a location that seemed perfect. I was very excited. I sent a letter to the New York City Health Department to request an inspection, because without their approval, I could not sign the lease. A couple weeks later, the inspector came and measured the square footage, informed me what repairs

needed to be done, and gave me the thumbs-up. Wow! Things were happening so fast. The landlord contacted his attorney, and soon after, I had the lease in my hands.

The lease was an eighty-page document full of words I had never heard before and sentences that made no sense whatsoever. I asked a friend of my mother's, who is a businessman, to review it and to let me know his thoughts, and a friend of mine gave me the number of a real estate lawyer. I quickly made an appointment to see him. Upon reviewing the lease, my lawyer and my mother's friend both advised me not to sign it unless significant changes were made. It turned out that I had no protection, and that the landlord had control over a lot of the clauses. I handed the landlord the lease with all the changes, and, much to my disappointment, he turned me down. I had become attached to that space and, needless to say, this was a huge setback for me.

For the next year, I experienced one disappointment after another. I had interviewed many teachers and found two who would be suitable for the job, but with no commercial space for the school, I could not hire them. All the work was done—now all I needed was the space. I kept looking week after week, and I made a few offers. Every time I got excited, though, I would find out that either the space did not pass inspection, the landlord didn't approve, or it didn't work out for various other reasons.

The Department of Education has two specific requirements: the space requires two exits on the

same level in case of fire, and the space needs to
be within three blocks of a playground. Now, this is
New York City, and for anyone who is not familiar
with this city, playgrounds are very hard to come
by. Manhattan is more for singles; at least it used
to be before September 11. After that terrible day,
more couples got married and started having babies,
and soon there was a baby boom. The city was not
prepared for the increased demand for preschools
and playgrounds. I'd realized there was a need, and
hoped that meant the chance of success was greater
than the risk of failure. But I was becoming very
frustrated, and I was saddened by the idea that I
might not be able to open the preschool after all.

So I made an appointment for a massage to help
me to relax. My back was killing me, my shoulders
were tight with tension, and my stomach was tied
up in knots. When I arrived at the wellness center,
the receptionist informed me that unfortunately my
masseuse had called in sick and that all the other
masseuses were booked. She suggested I try a Reiki
session, saying that it was very relaxing. I had never
heard of Reiki before.

In desperation, I accepted her suggestion. I had
no idea what it was all about, so I did not initially
trust the practitioner. During the session, I kept
opening my eyes, and when I saw her hands hov-
ering over my body, moving from left to right, up
and down, I thought to myself, *What is this woman
doing? What is this practice?* It looked very suspi-
cious to me. She did not touch me at all, and at
times, she would yawn. So I thought she was bored,

but it turns out that Reiki relaxes the practitioner as well.

After the session, she told me that my stomach area had a lot of emotional blockage, and that she'd released everything and therefore I would be feeling much better. The next morning, much to my surprise, I woke up feeling much more relaxed, cheerful, and optimistic again, and in the next couple weeks, my feeling of being at peace grew. There were days when I felt still, as if my body was functioning in perfect harmony. I realized that Reiki had made me feel much better than massage did. From then on, I booked a Reiki session once a month. During the second session, I had more trust in the process, so I was able to close my eyes and fall into a deep sleep. For the past fifteen years, I'd had to go in for massages for my chronic back pain—sometimes the pain was so great that I could not sleep. But since starting Reiki, I had no more backaches. It was amazing! On the third treatment, I started getting curious about how Reiki works. I learned that the practitioner touches certain parts of the body that she/he feels need healing, and her/his hands become very warm and the patient feels the warmth. I became so curious that I decided to take a class. I was not interested in becoming a healer, I just thought it would help me to better deal with what I was going through. New York International Reiki Center (www .nyreiki.com) offered classes on the weekend, and I registered for the first available Level 1 and 2 class. Boy, was I in for a treat!

I went in with no idea of what to expect. "Good morning. My name is Mr. Budu and I will be your teacher for this class," he said. Among my classmates I noticed a woman who did not seem to fit in. I concluded that her energy was completely shut down and wondered if she would stay for the whole class. Sure enough, she did not come back after lunch. For some reason, everyone in the class had the same feeling about her. One definitely needs to believe and be open to spiritual experiences to do Reiki.

Mr. Budu was a soft-spoken man who always had a smile on his face and great humility. The first exercise he did was called an *attunement,* which was used to open the fourth chakra (heart), sixth chakra (intuition), and seventh chakra (connection to the divine). When Mr. Budu opened my intuition chakra, I had a vision of an eye opening, which meant that my intuition had opened. When he cleared my heart chakra, I felt compassion, manifested as a warm, very loving feeling. I had never felt that before and was moved by the experience.

The second day of the class was also great. Mr. Budu informed us that we were going to learn to see auras. I was ecstatic! We practiced on each other, and lo and behold, I could see my aura. To think that, in Miami, I used to pay money to have my aura photo taken and now I was able to do it on my own for free. I was amazed!

Because of the attunements, my aura had changed from orange to blue, which meant that I had inner peace and wisdom. During the lunch break, I

went over to Mr. Budu's desk and summed up my frustrating situation of not being able to find a space for my preschool. He proceeded to tell me that the reason I was not able to achieve my goals was that there was something that needed to be healed first. In my head, I was thinking about my father.

When the afternoon session started, the teacher needed to demonstrate how to do a healing session on a patient. He asked for a volunteer and I immediately raised my hand. When I lay down on the table, I was a bit nervous but decided to still go through the process. Mr. Budu put his hands over my heart chakra and immediately said that he felt a reconciliation and forgiveness coming soon. I was happy to hear that, because it meant that after this reconciliation, there would still be a chance for me to open the preschool.

The Reiki class elevated me to a higher spiritual frequency. I became very sensitive to the noise level of the city. On some days, I could not bear to hear the sirens, and I lived all the way up on the eighteenth floor! I found myself closing the windows of my apartment in order to have some peace and quiet. I also felt the need to go away and commune with nature. I took the train to Fire Island and stayed there for a couple days in a quaint bed-and-breakfast. One of the perks of this beautiful island is that no cars are allowed. I rented a bicycle with a colorful basket in the front and, with a big smile on my face, rode around the island. I felt like a little kid; I was definitely in touch with my inner child.

This made a few days of the twenty-one-day detoxification period easier. During this time, the soul goes through a major shift and positive changes usually occur. I read that some people experience nausea and even throw up to purge the toxins from their bodies. Those people are primarily the ones who have not bothered to resolve many years' worth of issues. I was lucky that my body did not have a lot of toxins because I usually deal with my problems as they come up.

Not that I was completely free of issues. My grandmother had passed away five years earlier. She was a sweet lady with a lot of love to give, and I was very close to her and loved her dearly. I'd made all the arrangements for the funeral but did not have the strength to attend the ceremony. And since I believe that my grandmother's spirit is watching us, part of me felt like I didn't need to go to the cemetery to say good-bye. Furthermore, I was very scared of cemeteries—just the thought of them made my knees shake. Every now and then my mother would ask me if I wanted to go with her, and my answer was always no.

But during the detoxification period, I woke up one morning feeling completely at peace and decided to visit my grandmother's grave. I took the subway to the cemetery, and when I found her grave site, I fell to my knees and began to cry. I asked her to forgive me for not visiting sooner. I looked around the cemetery and said, "So this is what will become of all of us." Perhaps by going there, I was trying to come to terms with my fear of death. When you

think about it, no matter how much we know about life, death will always be the greatest mystery that God has bestowed upon us.

Around that same time, I had a dream about forgiving my uncle. My grandmother was living with him before she died, and he was dating a woman whom my grandmother did not approve of. She told me one day during lunch, "This woman is not good for him. We have to keep an eye on her." I met the woman a couple times and came to the same conclusion.

When my grandmother passed away, my uncle was devastated because he, too, loved her very much. He was probably afraid to live alone, and so he proposed to his girlfriend. They got married three months after the funeral, which I thought was too soon. The rest of the family was appalled by his actions. Since the wedding, we had not spoken, even though my uncle lives in an apartment down the hall from my mother. I'd seen him in the elevator a few times but did not say a word to him. After the dream, however, my heart was open for forgiveness, and my uncle and I finally broke our long-standing silence.

One afternoon, I was listening to music, when all of a sudden I felt a wave of sadness come over me and I needed to look at my photographs from my time in Miami. As I looked at each picture, I reminisced about my two years there, and a couple tears rolled down my cheeks. Finally, I closed the photo album and, two minutes later, joy came back to my soul. It was a brief moment that made me accept my disappointment about not being able to live in

Miami for good, and I released all of my sadness and healed.

All those healing experiences made me eager to attend the next Reiki class to become a Reiki Master. It is recommended that the Master class be taken at least six weeks after the completion of Levels 1 and 2, because the body needs to adjust to the new energy frequency. Some people feel they need a year between the two classes. There are no set rules. I felt ready. I thought: *the faster I do this, the faster I can accomplish my goals and find the space for my preschool.*

During the Master Reiki attunement, my hands became very warm and I felt my body tingling all over. I noticed that when Mr. Budu asked us to choose between focusing on healing or manifestation of goals, I always chose manifestation, which meant that I was done with the healing part.

The next exercise was called "psychic debris clearing," and I again volunteered. Mr. Budu asked me, "Do you have a specific area in your body that you want to work on?" My stomach had been hurting for the past couple weeks. I'd tried to heal it myself but the pain was still there. I answered, "My stomach."

He continued with another question: "What color do you see around the problem area?"

I closed my eyes and responded, "A faded yellow."

Mr. Budu demonstrated the way this exercise is to be done, and when he finished, he looked at me and said, "And now what color do you see?" When I closed my eyes, I was surprised to see the color

purple! That meant that the connection to the divine had returned. I felt lighter, the pain was gone, and I was smiling. It was incredible.

When I woke up the following day, I was exhausted and emotionally drained. We had done a lot of work on our bodies. Good, positive work, but I felt like I needed to take it easy. In the late afternoon, my phone rang. Not recognizing the number, I debated whether to answer it or not, and I decided to pick up. On the other end of the line, a familiar voice said, "Hello." I realized then that it was my father! We spoke for an hour. That was a very long time for us, because communication was never his forte. I truly believe that, had he called me before the Master class, I would not have been open for that discussion because my heart chakra still would have been shut. So it was perfect timing—it was time to lay everything on the table. In the past, he became very defensive when I questioned him, but this time he was different. He listened to me and seemed to understand what I was trying to convey to him. We both came from a place of love instead of anger, and that made all the difference.

The following morning I was drinking coffee when I realized the importance of having a good relationship with my father, and I also understood how that connected to my past relationships with men. This reconciliation was the last piece in the puzzle of my healing. As I sipped my coffee and looked at the horizon, I knew that from that moment on, everything would be okay. And that I was going to find the perfect space for my preschool.

For the past five years, on my nightstand, I'd kept a photograph of a man and a woman kissing. In front of the picture, I'd placed two Chinese Baoding balls that my friend Bia had given to me as a gift. A yin-yang symbol was painted on each ball. For all this time, I had wanted to meet a man who was whole. The Reiki Master class helped move me toward wholeness, and I hoped that I would attract a man who was whole himself.

◆ ◆ ◆

CHRISTINA'S THOUGHTS

❖ If you have a chance, take Reiki classes. They don't require much of your time, and they will heal the deepest parts of your soul!

❖ Educate yourself on the stock market. Pick a couple stocks, then save and invest in your future by taking control of your finances and trading online.

❖ Buy only the necessities. It is possible to be happy with the simple things in life. And if you cut down on spending, you will have some savings for a nice, relaxing vacation. Isn't that better than buying yet another pair of pants that you really don't need? If you look closely, you end up wearing the same outfits anyway, even if you have a huge closet full of clothes.

❖ If you surround yourself with fun-loving people, their attitude is contagious and you will find yourself in a good mood.

❖ Write down changes you see in yourself. Your notes don't have to be long or formal—keep them short and simple. You will look back at what you wrote and find yourself smiling. Through your journey of growth, this will help you put the puzzle pieces together. And when you are whole and find your purpose, the pieces become a complete picture that is unique to each individual.

❖ Use only one credit card. Record your expenses daily—it will take you only a minute and will save you tons of time. Keep your receipts in an envelope in chronological order. It will be easier for you to check against the amounts on your bank statement.

❖ The most important key to happiness is your connectedness to the divine. If you are connected, you will move with the flow of the universe.

CHAPTER 7

Empowerment

In Athens with my grandmother, my mother, and Khalil.
I always loved Christmas with my grandmother.

A new emotion
An incredible sensation
Invades me
Listening to music
I'm scared
What's going on?
Am I in love?

I don't know
The moonlight
Penetrating the room
Gives an atmosphere
Warm and romantic
Maybe it's telling me
A secret
The silent moon
Moves life
But projects an irresistible tranquility . . .

A year had passed since I'd started taking the Reiki classes, and I had grown so much. But there was still a problem . . . I could not find a space suitable for the preschool! I started to feel down again. Would all my efforts be in vain? I just could not believe it. On top of that, I was becoming very anxious about my finances. I decided to start looking for a job, even though just the thought of it made me very sad. But I felt like I had no other choice.

I sent out about fifty résumés, then waited by the telephone. But no one called me. How could that be? I waited some more and then I felt that something was wrong. I had a good résumé, and I'd had plenty of decent jobs before. But this time around I was unable to get even one interview! Then I remembered Mr. Budu mentioning that he had an office outside the city. I called him to make an appointment.

Upon my arrival at his office, Mr. Budu sat me down in a comfortable chair and asked me what was wrong. As I explained my problem, I started to cry from my very soul. I had not slept for days, and I felt completely helpless and very much in the depths of despair. I'd done *everything* in my power to create my dream, but it seemed like it would always be just that—a dream. The vision was fading, the whole thing slipping away from me.

When the session ended and my tears had dried, Mr. Budu said, "Soon you will see your life change. You're going to be very surprised. Things will start moving." With those words, he gave me hope again!

The following week I went to visit my father in Virginia. During the train ride, I read Bill Clinton's *Giving*, a wonderful book about philanthropy, a subject dear to my heart. I felt very peaceful. The night before my departure, I'd had a dream that I was driving with my father up a very steep hill, and I was nervous. I looked up the dream in my favorite book of dreams, *10,000 Dreams Interpreted,* by Gustavus Hindman Miller. It said that the meaning of this was good if one reaches the top of the hill, and thankfully we had made it to the top.

It turned out to be a peaceful weekend, and I was glad to see my father after five years of estrangement. He had not changed much. I also saw his wife for the first time in fifteen years. In the past, I'd had so much anger and resentment toward her because, in my eyes, she had replaced me as my father's princess. She is fifteen years his junior, and I had read that if there is a fifteen-year gap between a man and a woman in a relationship, it means that the woman is subconsciously searching for a father figure to take care of her. It also indicates that the man is having a midlife crisis and wants to boost his ego and feel young again by finding a mate younger than his current wife. Indeed, when they got married, my father did take care of her and I was no longer his top priority. It had been hard to take, but that night at dinner, I put all my anger aside and accepted the situation. Once I did that, I felt free to move ahead in my life. I kept saying to myself during the whole visit, "I'm doing this for me; I want the hurt and pain to go away; I want to experience joy, laughter, and love again." And though my father was never a good communicator, he started to open up once he saw how important it was for me to be able to talk to him.

Since things were going well, I decided to show him the projections for my preschool and tell him about my dreams for it. In the past, he'd always been critical of everything my brother and I did, and instead of building our self-esteem, he would crush it. I'd always felt that nothing was ever good enough for him. Now, at first, the negative statements started pouring out. But I just let them go in one ear and out the other. I accepted that my father would always be like that, that this was his belief system, and I was not going to be able to change it. I needed to go on with my project and take responsibility for my actions.

There is a story circulated on the Internet that I took to heart. In it, there were a group of frogs who were part of a race to reach the top of a tower.

Of course, because the frogs were so small, no one thought they would be able to do it. The spectators jeered the frogs, saying they would never be able to make it and the frogs were surely too small to make it to the top of the tower. The frogs—stymied by the tower—started to give up. Eventually only a few frogs were left, trying to climb to the top of the tower. And then there was only one frog left. That frog kept trying and trying, and finally made it to the top of the tower. Everyone wanted to know what his secret was—how did he make it to the top of the tower? Finally, his secret was revealed: the little frog was deaf.

The moral of the story is: Never listen to other people's negativity or pessimism. Don't let them take your most wonderful dreams and wishes away from you—the ones you have in your heart! Always think of the power words have, because everything you hear and read affects your actions!

I came back to New York City with a great sense of accomplishment. I had reconciled with my father! It felt good to close this chapter once and for all. And suddenly a shift happened. My father started calling me and finally became supportive of my dream. That meant a lot to me. Of course, in the back of his mind, he was probably still hoping that I would get a stable nine-to-five job with good benefits instead, but at least he conveyed his support on the phone.

In the days that followed, something incredible happened. Two commercial spaces opened up. Not one but two! For a whole year, I could not find anything and all of a sudden, I'd found two perfect spaces! It was wonderful. My spirit lifted again, and I felt motivated and driven. *This is it,* I said to myself. *One of the two spaces has to work out.* While I was negotiating the offers, Karen, a good friend of mine who lives in Atlanta, came to New York for a visit. I was really glad to see her after a long time of not being able to connect. We spent a day together, and she told me all about her new venture and how she was struggling with the marketing aspect of it. Up to that point, I had not thought about a marketing strategy for the preschool. She explained the feeder system to me and gave me a couple of other ideas. After she left, I wondered if Karen had been sent to me on purpose to deliver that valuable information.

With that, a new idea popped into my mind: red, blue, and white uniforms for the kids! I felt that the jigsaw puzzle phenomenon was still going strong and getting me closer to the creation of the preschool. I also reviewed my budget to see where I could cut costs. One day, walking by a Home Depot, I decided to go in and look at wood samples and other materials I needed for construction. I wanted the classroom to look simple yet elegant, and I found a lot of materials at good prices. I then went on the Home Depot website and read the reviews, which I advise everyone to do because they will give you a sense of the quality and durability of what you want to purchase. I picked the materials that had five stars and excellent reviews, and you know what? The prices were very low. That was how I cut my construction budget in half.

Finally, one rainy morning, I received the answer to one of the offers I'd made on the spaces. Unfortunately, the news was not good: I would need more funds. The Realtor told me that if I came up with more money, the landlord might reconsider. I felt very frustrated and did not know what to do. My dream was within reach—I *had* to come up with a solution. So I went to see Mr. Budu for another session. I told him that he'd been right, and a lot of things had started to move after I last saw him. But I still had a major problem: my finances.

The answer he gave me shocked me. "You are not ready," he said. *Not ready?* I'd been working night and day on this project! I nearly walked out right then, but before I could, he continued. "When you are ready the money will come to you and all obstacles will be cleared. You are not ready, my dear." *I give up!* I thought, mad at God and everyone else. Is it going to take another ten years for me to be ready? And just what exactly does "being ready" mean? I was, to say the least, confused.

That night I crawled into bed, curled up in the fetal position, and cried myself to sleep. I dreamed that I was climbing a wall. I had all the right gear, the harness, and everything else. I had a little more left to climb but froze right before I got to the top. I did not back down. I just stayed there. Then I woke up.

Still in a bad mood from the upsetting news of the day before, I decided to take a walk to clear my head. I love walking in Central Park, away from the traffic and noise of the city. On my way back home, I felt a pull to go into a New Age bookstore. As I was browsing and wondering what I was doing there, my head turned up and my eyes stopped on a book stashed in the corner. The book was *The Success Principles* by Jack Canfield, author of the Chicken Soup for the Soul series. I could not reach it, so I asked a salesperson to help me get it down. I had the intuition that I needed to buy it, and so I did.

In one of the chapters, Mr. Canfield wrote about how, sometimes when we enter upscale stores, we feel like we don't fit in, and that we need to stretch our financial comfort zones. And there . . . right there . . . I had a huge breakthrough. Even though I was brought up with wealth, I always felt uncomfortable with brand names and hated to go shopping on Madison Avenue. Coincidentally, a couple weeks earlier, I'd received a Chanel wallet as a present. I'd switched my old wallet for the new one, and for a week, every time I took out my Chanel wallet to pay for something, I felt very uncomfortable, even covering the Chanel emblem with my hand. I did not understand my behavior and decided to go back to my old wallet. That chapter in *The Success Principles* reminded me of that incident. My exercise for the weekend was to get all dressed up, walk along Madison Avenue, and go inside every upscale boutique. At first, I was hesitant, but by the time I had walked twenty blocks, my comfort level was much higher.

The next morning, I again switched to the Chanel wallet, and this time it felt good! What a difference. A week later, I returned to those same stores, only this time I tried on $10,000 Valentino dresses. It was so much fun! And when I paid my bills, I envisioned money coming back to me as well. That was powerful! Whenever I wrote down "I want" statements, I'd catch myself, cross out "I want," and replace it with "I will." And, previously, I'd always been afraid to carry more than $20 in my wallet, so I chose to add $200. Something incredible happened the next day: my business line of credit was raised to the exact amount that I needed in order to be approved for the space. AMAZING! All that by shifting my energy and stretching my financial comfort level. My desires were no longer just desires anymore—they were commitments I'd made. My new behaviors provided me with more strength and faith than I could possibly have imagined prior to reading *The Success Principles*. I tried to apply these changes to my preschool vision. I loved one space more than the other—the location was ideal and everything seemed perfect. But I was scared of being disappointed again. One night, before I went to sleep, I detached myself from it. I thought to myself: *I need to let it go. If it is not meant to be, then I will accept that.* I again saw the power of surrendering. Detaching ourselves is the best thing we can do. But it is not easy!

I understood that being grateful is part of being successful, so I started a gratitude journal. I also knew that loving oneself and feeling worthy of wealth is part of success, so I did "the mirror exercise." Every morning, I would look in the mirror, smile, hug myself, and say, "I love *me*; I deserve abundance and success. From now on I will attract prosperity, joy, fun, and excitement in my life."

Now that my finances were in order, I was sure everything was going to be fine. Then I was turned down by both spaces. I could not believe it! I asked God in desperation, "Why? What more do you want from me?" I did not sleep that night from crying. Sure enough, God answered me through my intuition: I felt the urge to go away. But not simply on vacation, to swim and get massages and to relax . . . No, this would be another type of getaway.

I researched spiritual retreats in Sedona. I knew that was where I should go, and I found a retreat that offered exactly what I was looking for: personal growth sessions. I reserved a room and booked my flight for the next day. As the taxi pulled into the sun-warmed driveway, I was surprised to see that the retreat would take place in a quaint little house. I walked in and immediately felt comfortable in the two-bedroom home, decorated to give a cozy feeling. Shortly after my arrival, the owner and practitioner, Caroline, greeted me. Before we began my spiritual healing sessions, Caroline asked me to write on one piece of paper all the things that I did not want in my life anymore, and on another piece of paper all that I desired.

Then, in front of the fireplace, she smudged me and told me to throw the paper with everything I did not want into the fire. The paper burned as Caroline said a Native American prayer, and with that, I released my past and made room for my future.

We then moved on to an EFT (Emotional Freedom Technique) to clear out pending issues with my father. I needed to stand up to him and not worry so much

about his approval. His opinion about the preschool did not matter. It was my life, after all, and I was old enough to know what I was doing. Then Caroline and I had a hypnotherapy session. It was the first time I was hypnotized, and I did not know what to expect. She planted positive "seeds" into my subconscious; I was curious to see if my brain would remember everything from when I was asleep. But Caroline assured me that I would start changing things in my life without even thinking twice about it.

At dinner, I asked for a Coca-Cola. A wide-eyed chef said, "I am very sorry, but we only serve organic juices. Sodas are not good for the stomach." I was disappointed but drank water instead. The salmon and vegetables were delicious. This was a wonderful reinforcement of my growing habit of eating more vegetables and more healthy and organic foods, and generally being more aware of everything I ate.

In our next EFT session, I told Caroline that I'd had enough of trying to swim upstream. We replaced my struggles with our own version of the song "Row, row, row my boat gently down the stream . . . merrily, merrily, merrily, merrily . . . my life's an exciting dream!" She told me that, from now on, my life would be easier, and things would evolve naturally and fast. I was glad to hear that!

Next, Caroline took me and two other people to the medicine wheel, where she sang a Native American prayer and called on our spirit guides to help us. The medicine wheel was a circle with four direction points made out of stones. The south was the spiritual realm, the west was the emotional realm, the north was the physical realm (abun-dance), and the east was the mental realm and new beginnings. As we entered the circle, each person stood in one direction. I started with the south, and I found myself blurting out that I want to live life to the fullest and have *la joie de vivre*, then I walked to the west and, as if on its own volition, my voice said, "I want to align myself with purpose." I walked to the north and the same voice, louder and with more confidence than before, said, "I want abundance of success and wealth." Finally, I walked to the east and said with a big smile, "I am love, unconditional love to all beings." When each of us had gone around the circle, we shared our experiences.

I told Caroline that I'd been unconscious of what I was saying, but that everything I'd said was exactly what I wanted. She then told us that the medicine wheel mirrors what's going on internally, that it is the manifestation of our internal dialogue.

One morning, I was feeling energized, so I decided to hike up to one of the nearby vortexes. It was sun-rise by the time I got there. I started climbing the hill when I saw two arrows pointing in different direc-tions. One pointed up a very steep hill, and the other pointed to a hill more accessible for average hikers. I decided to do the steep hike. I started climbing the hill but soon got scared and walked back down. Two minutes later, I started climbing it again. In my head, a voice was telling me, *This is good! If you get to the top, you will overcome all your fears!* So I kept on putting one foot in front of the other, saying, "I

am overcoming my fears; I am overcoming my fears,"
as my heart pounded in my chest.

As I looked down into the valley, negative thoughts
came into my head. Thoughts like: *You could fall
and die*. Then positive thoughts would rush in and
replace the negative ones. Thoughts like: *You can do
it*. And I did! When I arrived at the top, my legs were
trembling with fatigue. I sat on a large rock, and,
with my hands raised to the sky, I thanked God that
I was still in one piece and said, "I did it! I am the
queen of the world!" Needless to say, I was ecstatic.
I sat there for two hours in pure silence. The sun
was rising behind the rest of the vortexes, and the
peace that I felt from that silence was indescribable.
I wished I could do that hike every day, to experience
such blessed silence. I was very happy that the voice
had encouraged me to keep on.

In the next hypnotherapy session, Caroline said
softly, "Close your eyes and imagine you are in an
elevator. Press the button that has ten on it. Now
you are going down . . . nine . . . deeper . . . eight
. . . deeper . . . seven, you are way down . . . six . . .
relax . . . five . . . Your body is feeling heavy . . . four
. . . deeper . . . three . . . you're almost there . . . two
. . . you're asleep . . . one . . . You exit the elevator
. . . walking through a hallway you see several closed
doors on your left and on your right . . . open one of
the doors and go into the room."

Inside that room in my mind, I sat on a chair and
started laughing like I have never laughed before. I
felt pure joy. At the end of the session, I walked out
of the room and into the same hallway. However,

this time all the doors were wide open, which for me signified the arrival of new opportunities.

Next, I had a visualization session, and something very interesting happened. Caroline asked me, "What image do you see that symbolizes your feminine personality?"

"A pink heart with two little feet and two little arms," I responded quickly.

"What image do you see that symbolizes your masculine personality?"

"A red heart with muscular Popeye arms," I answered with a smile.

"Now, can you put the two together?" she asked as though holding back laughter. I visualized the red heart and the pink heart holding hands and walking down a beautiful path, both happy about joining forces.

And that's how I again moved toward wholeness. A very simple exercise that made a big difference. In the second part of the visualization session, we concentrated on my fears concerning the preschool. Somehow, buried deep within my subconscious, a fear was blocking me from going through with such a big project. Finally, after thirty minutes of exercises, I had a vision of myself signing a lease!

The following day, Caroline told me about the growing eco-friendly movement, and I decided to make the preschool eco-friendly. Of course, being in a city like New York, where I would not be able to build the school from the ground up or put up solar panels, the idea had its limits. I opted to buy "green" furniture and materials for the children. I

would install low-flush toilets and bamboo flooring and use nontoxic "green" cleaning products.

I returned to New York right before Thanksgiving. It seemed like everyone was in a holiday mood, and it reminded me how festive our house had been around the holidays when I was growing up. But after my parents got divorced, seventeen years earlier, my mother stopped decorating the house, and we no longer bothered to put up a Christmas tree. Every year, I mentioned that I would like to decorate a Christmas tree, but neither my mother nor I got around to it. Something must have happened in Sedona, because that holiday season, I finally bought a Christmas tree and decorated it with beautiful ornaments, and I was in good spirits because the house looked festive again. My mother was very surprised and excited as well. I felt like our family had healed from the trauma of a bitter divorce and we were ready to have some holiday cheer again.

I also felt another effect of the medicine wheel a week after my return. I was emailing my broker about a space when I experienced a flash of inspiration and created a signature with Le Petit Paradis, Corp., the address, and the telephone numbers. I was no longer just Christina Houri—I was "Founder and President." I understood then why I had said out loud that I wanted to manifest my purpose when I was standing in the west part of the circle. My emotions up until then had not been aligned with my purpose. Creating the signature showed me that I had resolved my subconscious fear. And when I'd stood in the east and said that I am love, I'd become free of anger, full of love for everyone. Suddenly, I was ready to embrace people whom I was not on good terms with. Nothing that they did in the past mattered; I loved them unconditionally.

◆ ◆ ◆

CHRISTINA'S THOUGHTS

❖ Start a gratitude journal. I can assure you that you will feel your soul light up! I think it is the best antidote to depression.

❖ Laugh. Don't take life too seriously, and get in touch with your inner child. I recommend reading *The 100 Simple Secrets of Happy People* by David Niven.

❖ Take time to meditate. I cannot say that enough. Meditation will keep you connected to your spirit and open your eyes to your soul.

❖ Love and support your children, and do it with all your heart. It will connect you to each other in more ways than one. They will be more open to talk to you and feel safe that you are on their side.

❖ Walk as much as you can. Walking is a wonderful overall exercise that is easier than going to the gym and great for emptying your mind.

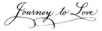

❖ Have the courage to reach for the stars. Little by little, step-by-step, you will make it. I promise.

❖ Last but not least, FIND YOUR SOUL AND PASSION AND FOLLOW YOUR HEART NO MATTER WHAT ANYONE TELLS YOU!

CHAPTER 8

Realization

Graduation day at Le Petit Paradis, June 29, 2012.

A festival of life
Exuding happiness
Colorful, bright and hopeful
Light as feathers
A wind flying
Passion
Wanting to burst
Loving as can be

Fiery and playful
That's the festival of life.

After the holidays, my broker called me with a great
space. Everything from that point on went fast. The
contractor met with me right away. The meetings
with the landlord concerning the lease were productive. We came to terms on everything without a lot
of negotiations. We had a meeting of the minds, and
everyone got what they wanted and everyone was
happy. I could not believe that I was rowing my boat
down the stream with an ease that I had never experienced before. By feeling more confident and more
joyful, one becomes a magnet for great things.

I signed the lease on a beautiful winter day. I
was now ready to start, and I was adamant about
doing everything myself. I wanted Le Petit Paradis to
be one of the first green preschools in New York City,
and it was. I chose and assembled the furniture
single-handedly—every single item at the school I
picked with care, from the teachers to dress-up cos-
tumes and every tiny detail in between. In my mind
I had an image of a jungle mural for the wall, so
I hired an artist to paint the scene. My preschool
reflected me, my personality, my sense of perfection, my professionalism, and all that I stood for. My
heart was the school; it was my cherished project,
my baby, my passion; and I nurtured it with all the
love I had. Everything had to be perfect, and it was.

Of course, like any new business, Le Petit Paradis hit some bumps in the road. What really helped was having Reiki sessions once a month with a wonderful woman named Jill, whom I'd found by chance. (Of course, we know by now, there are no coincidences.) During a session, I was feeling particularly down. So I kept saying the mantra: "I believe . . . I believe . . . I believe." For the first half hour, I repeated it in my mind. When Jill turned me over to work on my back, a song popped in my head. In my mind, I sang "I Believe I Can Fly."

After the session I felt much better and more optimistic about the situation. A couple hours later, I opened my mail and there was a new credit card with an image of a mountain, a person with open arms standing on its peak. The caption read: "I am triumphant!" All I can say is that it was a wonderful sign from the universe. Jill had told me to buy a couple of Bach flower essences and to sip them during the day if I had a setback. She must have had an intuition, because, the following week, I did have a setback and I needed the remedy! I went to Whole Foods and bought Mimulus, which brings courage and calm so that you can face things that worry you, and white chestnut, which encourages a peaceful and calm mind when thoughts and worries go round and round in your mind. Bach flower essences work like magic. If you have not experienced them, I definitely recommend them.

I was anxious because the economy was slowing down, and I did not want that to affect my business. I did a visualization of the registration list becoming longer and longer. I *really* focused on that list. First, the names came to me and I wrote them down in pencil in my mind, then I said: "No . . . pencil means they are not confirmed." So I erased the names and wrote them in pen. The last name, however, came to me in bold, with all the letters in caps. So I said to myself, "Hmm . . . This is going to be someone important, like someone from a famous or high-profile family."

I also trusted that clients were on their way, and I actually saw myself standing in line at Bank of America with checks to deposit in my hands. Sure enough, I had the exact number of registrations that I had visualized, and a celebrity did sign up! That was a great example of the power of visualization.

Le Petit Paradis Preschool opened on time, with more students than I could have ever imagined!

With school in full swing, I was now ready to work on my personal life. I wanted to share my life with someone and to have more balance. One Monday evening, I went to yoga class at a new center. While waiting for the class to start, I sat next to a small table with cards and pamphlets spread out on it. My hand reached out and picked up a few cards. One of them was for Sarah, a hypnotherapist. Her card had a spiritual caption on it that captured my attention. I found myself calling that hypnotherapist the next day and making an appointment to see her.

The intention of my first session was to attract the right man into my life. I closed my eyes and heard Sarah's voice telling me to go down the stairs from the tenth floor, down to the ninth, then eighth

floor, deeper now to the seventh floor, relaxing more and more to the sixth floor. My breathing slowed down drastically when I reached the fifth floor. By the fourth floor, I was completely relaxed and ready for the third floor. On the second floor, I had no awareness of outside reality anymore. Sarah said, "As you walk onto the first floor, you see a beautiful path with flowers along the way. Start walking on that path, feel the light breeze, the sun shining. You reach a pond, and you sit on a large stone." At one point, I heard Sarah's voice saying, "The man that you want to attract is kind." Right then, I began to cough, the fit lasting for a good minute. Going back up the stairs to consciousness, I was alone. When the session ended, she pointed out the coughing, and I realized that it was because I had a hard time accepting kindness from a man.

The second session was even more interesting, and the intention was to attract more financial abundance into my life. We did the same routine. Toward the end, when I started going back up the stairs, I saw myself wearing a beautiful dress and a tiara with a train made from money! I had a big smile on my face as I held my head high with the train flowing out behind me, feeling confident and highly esteemed.

During my third hypnotherapy session, I wanted to revisit attracting the right man, to see if there were any remaining issues to work on. To my surprise, the session was very romantic. Walking along the path of the first floor into my subconscious, I saw a tree. I sat under it and, leaning back and allowing the trunk to completely support me, I felt ready to be open and to receive. A man approached me. He was holding a bouquet of flowers. He gave me the flowers, and I accepted them with great joy. Then we danced cheek to cheek, the hills spreading their beauty before us. Suddenly, I saw a table set with candles in the middle of a field. We sat down to dinner and ate, laughing and talking for hours. At the end of the meal, he offered me the most beautiful necklace and, again, I accepted his gift with great joy. We then flew in his private jet to the beach. He held me, and in silence we both looked out at the moon shining its magnificent light on the ocean, together absorbing all that had just happened. This time, on my way up to the real world, I was not alone. I saw both of us in what looked like a ballroom from the nineteenth century. He was dressed in a tuxedo and I was in a ball gown, and we walked up the stairs together, arm in arm. For the first time in my life, I felt like Cinderella.

My fourth session was about harmony in the workplace. There was a lot of tension between me and the teachers at school, and I could not bear it any longer. I normally could hear Sarah's voice planting the intentions into my subconscious, but during this session, I went to sleep, and when I woke up, I could not remember anything at all. I was disappointed, thinking that it had been a wasted session. But the next day something incredible happened. The teachers became very respectful and, inexplicably, harmony was restored. I knew then that the session had worked.

My fifth session focused on my social life. My business was on a roll, and now I was ready to make new friends and go out more. Back in the field of my subconscious, I leaned once more against the same tree and became open to meeting my new friends. I then saw myself walking into a room where everyone was cheering and raising their champagne glasses in a toast to me. They all wanted to meet me. Walking back out to the field, I felt that even the trees wanted to converse with me. I felt appreciated, respected, esteemed, needed, and confident. Going up the stairs, I was beaming.

My sixth session was about laughter. I had become serious in the last few years and had lost some of my spirit of laughter. In the underworld, I saw a swing. I sat on it and started flying higher and higher, feeling lighter and lighter. I started laughing hysterically. I saw myself at the age of seven, running through the fields, my kite flying in the wind behind me. Then the Three Stooges came to my mind and I started feeling very goofy. Going back up the stairs, I was making funny noises and laughing all the way. I had reconnected with my laughter spirit.

For my seventh session, we focused on trust. As I entered the path on the first floor, I became a ballerina. I started twirling and turning, feeling more and more carefree. I arrived at a pond and saw the reflection of my smiling face on the water. That session was very sweet with an ethereal feel to it. I heard a message: "Be happy."

A couple weeks after that Cinderella session, I received an invitation to a gala. Normally I would not attend a fund-raiser if I did not have a date. But this time I felt compelled to go by myself. I bought a gown and hired a car service. On the way to the Plaza Hotel, I truly felt like Cinderella and wondered how my evening would end. Like the fairy tale, the ballroom was grand, and I felt on top of the world. It was a magical night. Sorry to disappoint you, but I did not meet my Prince Charming that night.

The next morning, I became very curious about the meaning of Cinderella beyond the actual story. I typed the word "Cinderella" into my search bar. (Ah! That Internet . . . What would we do without it!) I did indeed find something very interesting: the word "Cinderella" has become analogous to one who unexpectedly achieves recognition or success after a period of obscurity and neglect, sometimes applied to a person or group that undergoes a sudden trans-formation, such as an athletic team that loses fre-quently and then starts to win steadily. I understood then what Cinderella meant for me: I was that kind of person as well. It was definitely an "aha" moment!

A couple weeks later, I received an email from an astrologer about the Age of Aquarius and how there would be six eclipses during the year that would propel Aquarians forward in their lives. I am an Aquarian, so I followed her directions for creating a ceremony table. It was my first time doing some-thing like that.

Here are some guidelines for how to do a ceremony:

* Set up an altar to focus the energies. You can use a pretty scarf or napkin as an altar cloth.

- On the altar, place items that are meaningful to you such as candles, crystals, flowers, or figurines of spiritual beings.
- Start the ceremony with a prayer, or call in spiritual helpers according to your beliefs, such as Mary, Jesus, Buddha, goddesses, etc.
- Quiet your mind and visualize a balance between your yin (moon) energy and your yang (sun) energy. Draw your focus to each item separately and pray, chant, or state the intentions you have for each one. If you have compiled a list of things to release, you may want to burn it. Give thanks that your new intentions have already begun to manifest in the energy field, and open yourself to receive them on the third dimension.
- End the ceremony with a prayer for the healing of Mother Earth and for all beings on our planet. This is an excellent time to send prayers to the leadership in our country and visualize a world of peace, freedom, and unity.

Here are some suggestions for items and what they might represent:

- A written list of what you want to release
- Your bold intentions for the future
- Optimism in the form of a toy or whimsical item
- Compassion in the form of a spiritual figurine (the goddess Quan Yin is often used in feng shui)

- ◆ New thinking in the form of a motivational or spiritual book whose principles you want to embrace
- ◆ Equality and love in relationships in the form of a heart-shaped stone or rose quartz

◆ ◆ ◆

A couple months later, I went to Europe on vacation. There, I had a massage with a very interesting lady who told me about crystal healing. I was curious to learn more. She explained that the session involves surrounding the body with crystals. The person lies on the bed for one hour, relaxing while the crystals do their work, a ritual often referred to as a "crystal bath." Some people experience visions, colors, even soul traveling. She knew someone who did this crystal healing, but unfortunately, the practitioner was not available that week. I was a bit disappointed and thought that it was not meant to be. But upon my return to the States the next week, something very freaky happened. I received an email from a healer (I am not sure how he got my email address, but the universe works in mysterious ways) advertising his services, and on the top of the list was . . . crystal healing. I could not believe it!

I called him right away and made an appointment. I still felt like my life was all about work, and I really wanted to meet the love of my life. The session revealed to me that I needed to open my heart more and be more relaxed about it.

I had gone to the session without makeup and wearing sweatpants and sneakers, so I was not feeling particularly sexy. As I was walking back to my apartment, a young man looked me right in the eyes and gave me the biggest smile I had ever seen. I could not believe it! At that moment, I knew that he was an angel sent from the universe to give me confirmation. The next morning, on the way to work, another man did the exact same thing. It was very strange, and another confirmation.

I emailed the healer about my experience and told him that I was shocked, that I could not believe it. His response was: "You could make it believable!" Was I really so closed off? I knew that for the past couple years I'd had to focus on opening the school, and that I must have completely shut myself off from the possibility of any man coming into my life, even though deep down that was what I really wanted. But my soul was still not open to it.

Something else happened after the crystal healing that I was not prepared for. I wanted to revisit my notes from the Millionaire Mind seminar that I'd attended two years earlier. I reread everything, and suddenly I started to find a lot of pennies again! I had the creative idea to put all the money I found in a jar so that I could watch it accumulate. I realized that I was increasing my financial energy level. Until then, the universe had provided me with a certain amount, but now I needed to receive more. Revisiting my notes must have triggered something, and it was very neat to see that happen. A week later, I went to Hermès, Chanel, and some other high-end stores and picked out which handbags I would buy when I could afford them. That was very powerful! I also found a list of different seminars offered around the world. One in particular struck my fancy. Something seemed to be saying: *You should take this seminar.* So I went online and signed up for one that was to be held in two months.

My mother had given me a Mother Mary pendant a few years earlier but, since I was not religious, it had sat unworn in my jewelry box. One day, I decided to wear it with an outfit I'd recently bought. I usually change my jewelry daily to match my outfits, but the next morning, I felt the urge to keep the pendant on. It was very odd that I did that, but I trusted and followed my intuition. The next week, curiosity got ahold of me once more, and I started to research the meaning of the Mother Mary pendant. What I found gave me chills all over my body.

As it turns out, whoever wears that pendant will be showered with miracles and blessings. There were endless stories of the grace that people had experienced throughout the years. I read a few of them and was very moved. I also found out that it was some sort of initiation to higher consciousness.

I found a key on the street one day and placed it in the jar of change. A key is a great omen because it represents opportunity. If I told you that a couple days later I found another key, you might not believe me, but it's true! And while I was on a roll, I also found a die, which I added to the jar as well, because dice signify luck—good or bad. I would like to think that it was good luck. It's easy to find pennies but

odd items like that are rare on the streets of New York City. I felt that they were all signs from the universe guiding me to a better life.

The following week, I had an urge to change my wardrobe and to buy new apparel as well as some fun new jewelry. One thing I really wanted was a purple top. I'd always hated that color and it was crazy that purple was the color that I now wanted to wear. I remembered how I could not bear to wear black after the Reiki training, and I'd found myself getting rid of most of my clothes because they were black. So something must have been happening to me involving the color purple, perhaps because purple is related to higher levels of spirituality.

I found a couple of purple tops and put one of them on right away. I felt great and, one rainy day, I found myself singing "Singin' in the Rain."

Three years earlier, I had decided to write a book. I'd mailed out my manuscript from Miami and had received a contract, but somehow it had fallen through. So, at that time, I'd dropped the book and instead concentrated on opening the school. But now I was again struck by the idea to publish my book. I had a feeling that I would be contacted by an agent, and this book would be published in due time because I'd written it with the hope that it would help a lot of people find their way and reach their highest potential.

I was experiencing many coincidences. I'd called a friend of mine to inquire about her husband's recovery from surgery. He was doing well, and somehow our conversation turned to spirituality. She told me that she was reading something about higher consciousness and living a magical life. I told her that I'd signed up for a program called the Wizard Seminar. She screamed and said, "That's what I am reading about in *The Way of the Wizard* by Deepak Chopra!"

So I took my copy of *The Way of the Wizard* from my library and began to reread it. Mr. Chopra explains: To be a Wizard is the freedom to escape the boundaries of space and time and to be our authentic spirits. Once we achieve that, life will become magical. There are seven stages of consciousness:

- Innocence
- Ego
- Achiever
- Giver
- Seeker
- Seer
- Spirit

I knew I was at the seeker level and was ready to get to the seer level.

At the seeker's level, we start giving out of love and compassion rather than ego. Our priorities change because we realize that death is coming, and we begin to no longer expect anything in return, not even gratitude. As my mother always says, "Do good and throw it away." At this level, we start experiencing synchronicity and the power of intention.

The seeker still lives between the two worlds of ego and spirit, though she has had glimpses into

the soul. Her experiences of synchronicity will eventually lead her to the seer level. At that level, the presence of silence is timeless and constant. When that begins to accelerate, it becomes part of the cosmic consciousness. When you know this, all that you intend shall happen and you begin to experience miracles! You will not have the need to control anymore.

That state of being is comfortable with death because spirit and death are the same. Rumi wrote, "Our death is our wedding with eternity." Mr. Chopra says that at the seer's level we start reading more poetry. Now I know why, a couple months before, I had the urge to buy poetry books, and I even started thinking about taking a poetry class. Before that, I had not felt ready to read those books, because I was still at the seeker's level. I also started thinking about how I could become involved in UNICEF and other great foundations to start my humanitarian service.

I decided to grade the past year so that I could see how much progress I'd made. My grade turned out to be an overall B. Going from F (which was 2006, the previous year) to B is not bad at all. I knew, though, that I wanted to achieve A+ grades the next year and the years after that.

The time came to finally attend the Wizard Seminar, which proved to be a miracle in itself.

So many changes in my life.

Every night before I sleep, I whisper: "Thank you, God, for this day. I am blessed with your support, guidance, and love. I am grateful . . . I am love."

Closing my eyes, I feel a sense of comfort and ease, knowing that my life is being taken care of by a mystical universe that wants the highest good for every human being on this planet.

◆ ◆ ◆

REFLECTIONS ON THE SCHOOL

After years and years of searching and praying and struggling and working, it felt as though my preschool was an instant success story. The school had several great write-ups, including an interview with the *Wall Street Journal*. I had one full classroom and planned to open the second classroom soon after. It was my pride and joy. The kids of a famous pop star attended my school two years in a row. I was very touched when one of those kids sent me a beautiful drawing because she was not able to attend the year-end graduation ceremony. I keep that drawing tucked away in my drawer.

I found an apartment in close proximity to the school, and I yearned for every sunrise. With a big smile on my face, I looked forward to greeting the parents as they dropped off their kids in the morning. Interacting with the teachers was instrumental to me. I was involved in every step of the way, thrilled to watch every three-year-old grow into a five-year-old ready for graduation. My school, with its bilingual curriculum, was the feeder to the French Lycée, and I was proud of that.

Staying connected to the parents meant a great deal to me, so I decided to share with them a book that was dear to my heart by Mark Nepo, called *The Book of Awakening*. It was my New Year's gift to the parents. I was disheartened when only a few of them reached out and thanked me. When I expressed my disappointment to Mom, she told me that my gesture was from the heart and that is all that counts. I was not to expect but to accept. Until that moment, I still did not understand. Another lesson to learn. What has meaning to me does not necessarily have the same meaning to others, a fact I remind myself of whenever I am faced with a similar situation.

At the end of each school year in June, I was already looking forward to meeting the newcomers and their parents in September. I knew, in my heart, that I was giving my all to the children, making sure that they graduated from Le Petit Paradis Preschool with memorable moments, ready for their bright futures.

Whenever I sit by myself and contemplate the school, I feel overwhelmed with emotion. I think about the annual school picnic in Central Park followed by the school graduation, how happy the children were playing together in the park, how the parents' faces lit up as they watched their children receive their diplomas.

Destiny interfered when I was diagnosed with colorectal cancer. I was blown away by the news, but I did not and could not give up. I had to live up to my dream. No one was going to take that away from me. The love and support I got from the teachers and the parents when I gave them the bad news was overwhelming. I had to face the reality, and I had to deal with the situation the best that I could.

At my desk at the school with an angel over my shoulder.
January 9, 2008.

I want to be remembered as someone who:

- ♥ Served or helped those who were in need
- ♥ Influenced people and felt the effects
- ♥ Did work that brought more truth and ethical behavior into the world
- ♥ Grew in wisdom, compassion, generosity, and kindness
- ♥ Brought people together
- ♥ Helped people reach their highest potentials

♥ Helped people grow spiritually toward
   wholeness
♥ Made a difference in someone's life—adult or
   child
♥ Communicated, inspired, enlightened,
   brought joy to human development
♥ Left a legacy

EPILOGUE

With Mom in Auntie Lynna's and Ammo Marwan's garden.
Palma de Majorca, August 18, 2009.

My Dear Beloved Mother,

I have written you poems of love when I was younger and given you cards of love when I got older. This morning I find myself overwhelmed with emotions of love for you.

You have been on this journey of life with me since my birth as a child and continue to be by my side on this journey of rebirth into spirit and miracles.

You are the sweetest person I have met. A true angel on Earth. I am forever grateful to have you as not only a mother but my friend, confidant, and of course traveling companion! ☺

I love you more than words can say. I will miss you when you are gone traveling, but I will always hold you in my heart as my treasure.

Be at peace my beloved mother, have fun reuniting with your friends and light up the world with your radiant spirit, for life is magical and miraculous for people like you.

I raise my green juice to you! ☺
Love,
Tina

• • •

To you, my beloved Tina,

I have NO words,
for yours struck my heart like a soft feather,
Caressing the veins that run through it,
Deeply touched, I will go on this journey of mine,
with you by my side,
knowing that the angels are protecting you,
you have become one angel yourself.
The transformation becomes you,
It lights up your face,
as your beautiful journey continues,
I will be by your side,
holding your hand as I fly away today.

You are here, I am there but we shall always be together,
bonded by our LOVE for one another.
—Elsi, Your Mother, Friend, and Angel

♦ ♦ ♦

Christina, my only daughter, left us and this world on August 19, 2014. She was forty-seven years old.

It was supposed to be "Our Year."

On January 1, 2014, Tina said, "The Year of the Horse starts Friday! It's our year: Mom's and mine!" Tina and I, celebrating life to the fullest. That day, freedom finally began—she was herself, and she felt free.

She had just moved to Miami. Sprawled on the grass, she said, "I am safe in the core of Mother Earth. I feel nurtured. I have let go of the past and my ego."

But after just six weeks in the sunny city, she never returned. "Our Year" to have fun and enjoy all life's pleasant surprises became a year of shattered dreams.

Tina didn't feel well. Her colorectal cancer had returned, unbeknownst to us, an unwelcome guest in her new home. After helping Tina move into her apartment overlooking the ocean, I stayed with her until two weeks before her February 3 birthday, when I had to return to New York for a commitment. Tina attributed her discomfort to the food she ate, but I wasn't so sure and wanted to change my travel plans. She insisted I go. Even as I left her in bed, I arranged to return a week later for a birthday surprise. Our longtime friends Gisele and Miriam were my accomplices.

She sobbed with joy when she spotted us, and she kept repeating that it was the best surprise of her life. Her beautiful smile resurfaced, and we celebrated despite her pain. After that, I stayed in Miami to take care of her. She refused to see a doctor until one evening when she could not take it anymore. She asked me to fly her to the emergency room in New York City. Dr. Fadi Attiyeh, her surgeon, and Dr. Gabriel Sara, her oncologist, were her doctors from her first cancer diagnosis in 2010. Tina wanted to be under their supervision, so we took the first plane out in the morning. The cancer had spread. She was supposed to receive eight treatments, but after the sixth treatment, she could not tolerate any more. She was too frail. I took care of her twenty-four hours a day, seven days a week, in my Lower East Side apartment. We did not want a nurse looking after her.

Tina was all about love, and she yearned for love and affection, something only family could give. Every night, with our heads touching and our hands intertwined, my daughter and I kissed each other good night and waited for sleep to creep up on us.

We cherished our silent hours, from 5 to 7 p.m. Later, she would lie on her tummy while I stroked her back, trying to comfort her.

"Mom, how can I stop the chatter in my brain?" she asked. When I inquired what she meant, she

said, "Nothing specific, but a lot of confusion in my head."

"Count down from one hundred to ten," I would answer. Every now and then she'd look up at a picture taken during her time working at Club Med—she's in a pink-fuchsia dress, her long blonde hair flying in the wind. She'd taped it on the wall facing her bed, like a beacon of hope. She prayed that one day, when she got better, she would be that person again, the person with *la joie de vivre*.

"Do not worry, Mom, I *know* I am going to be okay," she'd say. But nothing seemed to help: not the smell of burning sage or the touch of essential oils. Soon she spoke as though her spirit were crushed. "Where is my spirit now? I want to be that person who was carefree, joyful, and optimistic. Now, all that is a mirage, a dream!"

One day I was on an errand and saw a bed of beautiful pansies hugging a tree. I thought of Tina lying in bed, not able to enjoy the outdoors and the nature she so loved. I took a picture and sent it to her. When I returned, she thanked me for sharing it and for thinking of her. Then she said, "Mom, you know me well and you know that I am not jealous of anyone, but today, as I lie helpless in this bed, I am jealous of those walking in the streets."

Shortly after that, she made the decision not to have any more visitors. She wanted peace and quiet. She wanted to spend time praying, healing, and regaining her strength. She was becoming weaker by the day, but still she needed to work on her inner strength. She kept saying, "I lost the key to my joy, to my laughter, but I need to hold on tight to the key of hope." So she made plans to go to Sedona with her friend Maddalena, and with our friend Reem and me to the spa at the Peninsula Hotel in New York for a weekend. She wanted to continue living, so she continued planning. She also talked about our walks by the river when she had cancer the first time. Unconditional love and wanting to live in the moment were her salvation; they kept her from giving up.

"When are we going to laugh again like we used to?" Nothing and no one could make her laugh, let alone smile, except Jim, her acupuncturist, who became her good friend. She felt safe in his presence and he brought her comfort. She looked forward to his visits.

Images race through my head, like the one of a late afternoon when Tina, my son, Khalil, and I held hands as she said, "I want to live; I do not want to die." Then there is the image of Reem and me watching in silence on the other side of the bed as Tina and her brother held hands. Those were indescribable moments in time—intimate moments when everything in the world stood still. Those moments felt like a whole lifetime.

On August 13, she asked me to call 911 so that an ambulance could take her to the emergency room at Roosevelt Hospital. She texted her father, who met us there, followed by Khalil, then Reem and Maddalena.

The doctors told us it was a matter of hours. The hours turned to five days, with her hanging on to life. All along, she said that she was not in pain, just uncomfortable from lying in bed and the bed-sores. Having lost so much weight disturbed her a lot, and she kept repeating, "How did I get to be like this, so thin and so fragile?" She'd resisted taking medication because she wanted to be aware of what was happening. That's why it broke my heart to see Christina knocked out with morphine the afternoon she was moved up from the emergency ward to her new room. After that, I forbade the staff from giving her any pain medications. She wanted to be alert—voiceless but alert until the last minute. I am glad I kept the truth from her, because she was a fighter and I did not want her to give up. Only once, she expressed some anger toward God. "What more do you want from me, God?" she screamed at the top of her lungs. "Did I not suffer enough so far? Take me now if you want!" We were both crying our hearts out. That was the only time she saw me cry. I begged her not to repeat those words again. She replied, "Okay, okay, I promise to commit to my healing."

She never stopped reassuring me that she knew she was going to be okay.

Reem came by the hospital every morning to see her, and Maddalena was always by her side. Christina felt comforted by the presence of her dad and Khalil. I slept on a cot next to her. We agreed that she would shake her bed to wake me up if she needed anything. She had no idea that my eyes were wide open and sleep was nowhere in sight for me. On Sunday, two days before she left this Earth, she said with her disappearing voice, "If they do not make me feel better by Tuesday, I want to go home." At 2 a.m. on Monday, she asked me to write down some questions to ask her doctor when he came to visit her later that morning. When her doctor arrived, I had all of Christina's questions on a piece of paper. He told me that he had to be honest with her, to tell her the truth about her condition. So that she could let go.

He told her that the tumor was taking over and there was nothing anyone could do about it. "What tumor?" she asked, and then she was silent. At that point she realized there was no hope. She was quiet. When Jim came to visit her after the doctor left the room, she told him that she needed a big miracle. She yearned to hear the Native American rattle ceremony but knew that it was not possible in the hospital room.

On Monday night, both of us stayed awake, and I massaged her back, her legs, and her feet, as they were getting numb. When I stroked her forehead, she kept calling me "my angel." We did not sleep a wink; we just sensed each other's presence in total silence and avoided looking into each other's eyes.

Tuesday morning she whispered in Reem's ear what the doctor had told her the day before and then murmured, "It is not fair." Since her friend Maddalena was by her side, I wanted to run home for a quick shower and to change clothes, and Tina looked at me and nodded. I ran quickly out of the room as though escaping the inevitable. I came back at the speed of light. Her dad and Khalil were with her. Maddalena and I took turns stroking her hands.

I continued to avoid looking into her eyes. The afternoon seemed to linger on as Maddalena and I stayed with Tina; she did not want any nurses near her. She was shivering and asked me to cover her. "Am cold," she whispered.

Hours before, the nurse had pressed the heat button instead of the air-condition button so we had hot air, and Christina nodded that it was okay to keep it that way. She kept shivering and asking for more covers.

At her bedside, Maddalena faced her and stroked her hands. "My head is hurting," Christina whispered. I was by Tina's side, but I still couldn't look into her eyes. "Can I put my hand on your head?" I asked her. Little did I know this is where the soul comes out—the top of the head. She murmured, "I am dying, I am dying," with the most angelic look on her face.

At 7:45 p.m., she let out her last breath.

It was Tuesday, the day she'd said she wanted to go home. Instead, she went to her eternal Home. A piece of me left with her.

❖ ❖ ❖

My thoughts turn to memories of Christina throughout her life, from when she was a child all the way to her final moments: her graduation from the French Lycée of New York; attending the Fashion Institute of Technology; meeting Reem, who became not just a close friend, but more like family; traveling to Paris for an apprenticeship with Givenchy; her time working for Club Med, traveling the Caribbean—so full of life, happy, and carefree; the joy she felt working with children.

When Christina first went to Miami in April 1986 with me at the age of twenty, she fell in love with the city and said she wanted to move there one day. She finally did in 1992, again in 2004, and, for the last time, in 2014.

On that 1986 trip, we stayed in a beautiful hotel overlooking the ocean in Coconut Grove. It was there that she wrote one of my favorite poems. The ending sticks in my mind like glue: "Oh, how wonderful it is to be alive!"

She was passionate about life and living it to the fullest. She was forever grateful. She wrote, "Every night before I go to sleep I whisper, 'Thank you, God, for this day. I am blessed with your support and love. I am grateful. I am love.'"

After my divorce in 1991, Christina, Khalil, and I tried to remain close. It was a rough few years for us as a family. It was only then that we realized that life is all about surprises—pleasant ones as well as unpleasant ones. We also became aware that there were many lessons yet to learn, so we embraced confrontation. Life was not about living happily ever after.

I have a crystal-clear memory of the day in May 1992 when Christina made her decision to move to Miami the first time. She had applied for a job with Club Med. She waited a long while for an answer, and when she did not hear back, she packed her bags and moved there anyway. A few weeks after she arrived in Miami, Club Med offered her a managerial

job in their Martinique boutique. It was an offer she could not refuse, so she left Miami for life and work on the Caribbean island.

After her stint in Martinique, and until August 1996, she worked in Guadeloupe, Sandpiper, and Paradise Island. She was young and carefree, with a bright future ahead of her. Reem, Khalil, and I took advantage of the situation and visited her on the different islands. There she was her true self—bubbly, full of energy, happy, enjoying every moment. Her only plans were to live for the day. She thought she had plenty of time to pursue her dreams, one of which was to work with kids.

Then she'd had enough of the carefree Club Med life and headed back to New York. In September of 1996, she landed a job at a French bilingual preschool on New York's West Side. Finally, she was working with kids and loving every minute. She'd found her purpose, was taking classes on Montessori education, and building her life. She was determined to realize her dreams and make them a reality. After all, she believed in miracles and the power of intention. She stayed in that job until June of 1998.

Between 2000 and 2004, Christina had two administrative positions. The last one was in a bank as an assistant to the director. That job paid well, but she just wasn't content. "It's not me, and my heart is not in it," she told me. She could not work in a field that did not capture her heart and nurture her soul.

Her heart and soul were in helping others. Most of all, she wanted to spend quality time with

underprivileged children. She wanted to help provide a safe environment for them, to educate them
and help them build their self-esteem. That want
became a need that she had to fulfill.

She looked forward to the weekends, to her trips
to Harlem where she spent time with the children.
Deeply invested in helping them with their problems, during the week she planned solutions to take
with her the following weekend.

In September of 2004, she decided to try Miami
again. That was where her heart was, where she felt
free by the sea and the palm trees she loved.

It was then that Christina began writing this
book. She decided to call it *Journey to Love*. It was
to be everyone's journey, and this is why she laid
her heart out so fully. She bravely put down her
experiences, the most private and most intimate
ones, for everyone to read. She meant to share what
influenced her the most, and spirituality was on the
top of her list. She used her knowledge of Reiki for
self-healing, but also to help others to heal.

Unfortunately, this time around, Miami was a
disappointment and so was her job. She felt trapped
by yet another administrative position. She loved
her apartment at the Mirador-by-the-Sea, her walks
on the beach, and the warm weather. Still, all that
was not enough, so in June 2006, she headed back
to New York.

In 2008, after much soul-searching and two
years of hard work, she made her long-held dream
into a reality: she opened the doors of Le Petit
Paradis Preschool. It was wildly successful, and I

was so proud of her. Sadly, she had to stop running the school after cancer struck the first time.

We were in Portugal on vacation in August 2010. Christina had stomach problems the last few days of our trip. We attributed her discomfort to something she ate.

At the security line in Lisbon Airport, she bent down to pick something up. It was a cross with the image of Our Lady of Fatima. She kissed it, said it was a good omen, and tucked it in her bag.

Her case was later misdiagnosed as diverticulitis, or inflammation of the digestive tract, and she changed her eating habits. When the problem persisted, she opted for an MRI in January 2011. Results showed a mass. That was the beginning of our nightmare.

Christina was admitted to the emergency room, and after a series of tests, she was released.

It was February 3, 2011. An unforgettable day, Christina's birthday. We left the hospital with the worst news. I had planned a surprise lunch for her with some friends at one of her favorite restaurants. No one was in the mood so we all decided to go to her place instead. Reem ordered a delicious pink velvet cake and we "celebrated."

We all had to step into our new reality. After a series of treatments and two operations, Christina was declared "cancer free" but was expected to resume a long series of "preventative" intensive chemotherapy treatments. The unthinkable! She refused.

She chose the option of routine checkups every three months. She did not follow through, and said she was fine.

In August 2013, we spent five weeks in Cannes, where we rented a house in the hills. Our friends Soumaya and Ambara joined us. It was a blissful, sweet, and sour vacation. Christina proclaimed, "Ah, I love the South of France, St. Tropez, Cannes, Mougins. I am *me* here; my true spirit shines."

Christina burst into tears as I drove by the majestic bay of Antibes, overwhelmed with emotions. "Why are you crying?" I asked her.

"Tears of joy," she answered. I wonder now if it was perhaps a premonition, a fear that she might not return to that place.

Toward the second half of the trip, the cancer struck back. Christina kept having stomach problems and always blamed something she ate.

Back in New York, she was preparing for the coming school year with the help of the school director she appointed. She was confident that with the school in good hands, she could manage it from Miami. She would come to New York every few months for a few weeks to oversee it. "I want to keep the school until I turn sixty-one, create my foundation for humanitarian work, publish my book *Journey to Love*, start on my sequel *Living in Joy*, and travel," she said.

◆ ◆ ◆

I will always remember Christina's memorial on September 28, 2014. We started with a ceremony at the Greek Orthodox cathedral in New York, then went for an intimate gathering at Reem's.

Reem had two hundred long-stemmed pink roses in vases spread throughout the bright room. Everyone who attended was asked to take one rose to press within Christina's book, which you now hold in your hands.

Reem arranged for a vocalist to sing Christina's favorite songs: "Amazing Grace," "The Impossible Dream," "Somewhere Over the Rainbow," and "Smile" by Nat King Cole.

Everyone in that room was meant to be there, to gather to celebrate Christina's life and remember her with our hearts.

By reading this book, even her closest friends will know her more deeply and intimately. Sometimes we don't learn about the depth of one's soul until after they are no longer on Earth.

Why do we think more about those we love when they are gone, rather than when they are here?

Every morning I wake up to her voice saying in my ear, "*Buon giorno, Oummy*" ("Good morning, Mommy") and her radiant contagious smile, always from the heart, popping up to greet me.

With a huge lump in my throat and terrible grief, I have attempted to recount the nightmare of Christina's period of suffering—the nightmare that became a surreal dream after she left us.

I feel her presence daily.

I will forever think of Tina as traveling, and that I shall meet up with her somewhere soon. Travel was a passion we shared—we wanted to travel the world, and I constantly made fun of the list she kept of where and when we would go.

I wish for people to give death a different dimension. I feel sorrow, yes, but I shall resume celebrating Christina's journey through life, supported by her friends and mine.

Taking what I call "journeys" is how I show the world that those who "leave" us continue to embrace us and send us signs of their presence. Tina has sent us many. It is not all about people leaving. They remain. They fly. They are around us. That's what the journeys signify.

Christina's journey is everyone's journey. Tina will always live in my heart and her smile will forever illuminate my path. Her journey is a celebration of life! We do not need to live forever but we need to *live*, for precious moments are like rainbows; they escape if we blink.

Time floats within a universe that is obscure and hurried through by most. Once in a while, memorable moments breeze in from the cracks of our present. A breath of fresh air, a sweet aroma, a tingling chime. They warm our hearts, lift our spirits, and put a smile on our faces.

The importance of human relationships, to one another and to nature, is the essence of our existence. The expression of one is the reflection of the other. Therefore, life continues as an open-ended circle propelling us to the eternal light and to our eternity.

Central Park with the cherry blossom trees.

April 2013.

I AM FREE!

ACKNOWLEDGMENTS

FROM CHRISTINA:

I would like to thank my mother for her unconditional love, my brother, my friends, without whom I don't know what I would have done, and Mr. Levine for approving Pierre Marcel's art for my cover.

FROM ELSI:

Christina would have said, "From the bottom of my heart, a collective thank you." To Khalil (Lilo, as she called him), for his continuous love, dedication, and support. To my dear friend, Sally Farhat Kassab, for making her home my sanctuary and for being instrumental in assisting me to publish Christina's book, holding my hand through the process. To Paul Kassab, for giving Sally and me the freedom to turn your home into a workplace, including asking you to completely take over caring for the babies. To Stephen Kassab, the true gentleman, age eight, for reading "Lassie Come Home" to me every night.

After my working for hours while reliving Tina's final days, your young voice and presence soothed my drained soul. All of you: I cannot thank you enough.

To Reem (Reemo to Tina), our dearest closest friend, for being there every step of the way, appearing at the right time with the Greek Orthodox priest to bless us at the hospital as we held hands and prayed, and for writing the foreword to this book. To Maddalena Molli (Maddy to Tina), Christina's dear friend, for being at Christina's side when most needed and for staying at Christina's bedside at the hospital for hours on end, but, most of all, for sharing with me Christina's last breath. To Rana Bazzi (Raaana to Tina), for coming from Orlando and surprising Christina during her worst hours, listening to her low voice when her words were scarce, and for her courageous reading at the memorial ceremony. To Rima and Eddy Moghabghab, for their enduring support and for giving Christina a memorial she is most worthy of in Beirut, and my deepest appreciation to all the friends and relatives who shared in that memorial. To Margeret Daniel (Margo), for being the first person to send a contribution for this book. To Miriam Duhau (Mimi to Tina), for making a special trip from Miami to visit Christina during her last days, though she was not able to see her. I shall forever remember how Maddalena and Miriam stood by my side and helped me close Christina's Miami apartment in three days. To Lynna and Marwan Kalo, our dear friends, for sharing my most difficult moments despite their own grief after losing their own daughter, Myra, to cancer. The first

thing Christina wanted to do when she was told she was cancer free was to visit Lynna and Marwan in Majorca. She said, "I do not feel good that I am alive and Myra is gone."

My deep gratitude to Ellen Weldon, my dear friend, for printing Christina's *Created with Love* memorial booklet and for her labor of love calligraphy gift to this book.

Thank you to my dear friend and neighbor Linda Moeller, for faithfully standing by our side, massaging Christina's feet and tending her, for her support through my most difficult days, especially when Christina's ashes arrived at my door. To my buddy Talal Alazm, who accompanied me on my rattle ceremony mission for Christina in Sedona and who never hesitates to be by my side at all times. "Anything for Christina and you," he always says. To Toula and George Vlachos, for being my family.

To James Rohr (Jim to Christina), for making Christina smile when her smile was rare and for that Monday morning visit at the hospital one day before Christina left us. To Elizabeth White (Beth), for sharing Reiki practices with Christina and for her comforting sessions.

To Gisele Bathish (Gilo to Christina), for sharing that apparition in a cloud and for being Christina's *joie de vivre* role model.

To my cousins Helen Cools Lartigue and Cynthia Musallam. Your presence meant the world to me. Nathalie Berard, *un grand merci* for finding Christina's feathers.

To my dear friend Fidokia Nourcy (Fido to us), for flying in from Paris to be with us for the memorial. To Bia Rique, our dear friend, who flew all the way from Rio de Janeiro for the memorial. Thank you to Daniel Ozan, my dear friend from Buenos Aires, for surprising me at the church for the memorial mass. To my dear friend Alida Harb, who flew in from Saudi Arabia to share in our memorial. Thank you to dearest Aminy Audi, for holding my hand when I needed it the most. To Colette Astorgue (Coco to Tina), who flew in from Oregon for the day to assist in the memorial. To Lana El-Halabi, for leaving her babies in Providence to give me her warm hug in church. Thank you to Monsignor Jorge Quinones for blessing Christina's ceremony in the Venice lagoon.

Thank you to Esther, Chadia, Stephanie, and Francisco Batista for being our family. My deep appreciation to Saree Ptak for her legal advice and for her patience with the parents of the school-children. Thank you to my niece Michelle and her daughters Arien and Tabitha for their help, and my brother Suheil for his continued support. My deep gratitude to Pierre Marcel for giving us permission to use his image on the cover and to Stephanie Jalinos for sharing that magic day of meeting Pierre Marcel and Sabine Mrowe in Normandy.

My deepest gratitude to all the friends who attended the memorial mass at the Greek Orthodox cathedral and who assisted in the ceremony at Reem's home.

My profound appreciation to all those who sent warm messages and cards that touched our hearts from all over and in particular the children's parents from Christina's school. I raise my cup (as Christina would have said) to Kinda Younes for her enthusiasm toward Christina and Le Petit Paradis Preschool. Thank you to Vanessa Ghenania for carrying on with the school and keeping it alive under the name of Arc en Ciel.

I salute and raise my hat to all the friends who shared my journey in celebrating Christina's life after she left us.

Our heartfelt thanks go to Dr. Fadi Attiyeh, our family friend and Christina's surgeon, for his extreme care and kindness toward Christina and for making her comfortable in his presence at all times. Special thanks to Dr. Gabriel Sara for his perseverance and for taking the time to answer Christina's many questions and, most of all, for his speech at the memorial.

Last but not least, my deep appreciation to Karen Upson and the team at Girl Friday Productions for realizing Christina's dream to have her book *Journey to Love* published.

Special thanks for their generous contributions: Najah Ala'ali; Aminy Audi; Dr. Alida Harb; His Excellency Suheil and Rita Shuhaiber; Dr. Ramzi Daloul; Hala Fakhri; Ilham and Ghandi El Halabi; Maha, Marwan, and Misha Naaman; Maddalena and Aaron Wrattan; Luis da Cruz; Salim, Rene, and Rania Nassar; Cynthia Musallam; Helen Cools Lartigue; Dr. Peter and Eva Farha; Richard and Linda Moeller; Maria Kaknis; Pierre Dulaine; Nelly and Nicholas Choueri; Jean Rene and Shadia Clot; Mahmoud

and Nia Farshchian; Claud Fatu; Servin and Daniel
Beneat; Dr. and Mrs. Fadi Attiyeh; Fidokia Nourcy;
Michelle Lapas Kottara; David Gitel; Christine Lang;
Dr. Jacob and Evy Musallam; Carolyn Fischi; Esther
and Francisco Batista; Katherine and William Boyle;
Lana El Halabi and William Alvarez; Miriam Duhau;
Valerie Gelb; Rula, Layan, and Sireen Jawdat; Nadine
Hajjar; Maureen Kenny; Suhad Amin; Rana Halabi;
Gisele Bathish; Hala and Omar Gharzzedine; Lucy
Cavalcanti; Leann Stella; Dr. Denise Estefan; Kim
Ambrose; Lisa and Robert Braden; Margeret Daniel;
Stephanie Jalinos and Mathieu Dondain; Rima
Bordcosh; Penelope Wilder; Ori Ravar; Jean Dubno;
Nichola Hakim.

APPENDIX

Poems

A gentle soul

Loving and kind

For he knoweth

Of fear not

Life so sweet

Colorful and bright

Soul craving

For such a knight

To hold and protect thee

From all that is not right

Such passion from he reveals

So ready am I

For he with tears

For such happiness he will bring

And I to thee

Two gentle souls

Loving and kind

Living together

Forever in Peace.

◆ ◆ ◆

By the sea in Biarritz, France.

By the sea is where I feel free
Where I can think peacefully
By the sea is where I long to be
Let all my worries fly free . . .

◆ ◆ ◆

A man so romantic
A love so passionate
A bond so strong
A relationship so brilliant
A life so joyful together.

◆ ◆ ◆

To be in love . . . Ah! What a dream
For a woman who's always
Searching for perfection
Moved by her sensitivity

Deceived by its consequences
Wanting only to recapture her joy of life
Being only alone . . .
Will she try again?
Will she succeed?

❖ ❖ ❖

Sitting by the sea
Lovely sounds of seagulls singing
Beautiful they are
White
Sign of peace and tranquility
Looking to the horizon
Sailboats searching for treasures
Will they come back happy?
Thinking to myself . . .
Oh! How wonderful it is to be alive!

❖ ❖ ❖

HERE'S A BRIEF EXPLANATION OF THE CHAKRAS AND THEIR FUNCTIONS:

First chakra: Also known as the root. Base of the spine. Groundedness to the earth and seat of Kundalini energy.
Color: Red
Stone: Garnet

Second chakra: Lower abdomen. Home of sexuality and creativity.

Color: Orange
Crystal: Tangerine quartz

Third chakra: Solar plexus. Self-confidence and
willpower.
Color: Yellow
Crystal: Citrine

Fourth chakra: Heart. Compassion. Governs the
heart and love relationships.
Color: Green
Stone: Emerald

Fifth chakra: Throat. Communication. The seat of
your true voice.
Color: Blue
Stone: Lapis

Sixth chakra: The third eye. Sixth sense. Intuition
and guidance from your spirit.
Color: Indigo
Stone: Azurite

Seventh chakra: The crown. Understanding,
knowing, consciousness, connectedness to the
divine. Living from purpose.
Color: Violet/White
Crystal: Amethyst

◆ ◆ ◆

The colors of the aura are associated with specific abilities or qualities. Here is a brief description of a range of colors for your reference:

Red: Activity, extroversion, movement, vitality, health, joy, passion

Dark red: Vigor, willpower, masculinity, leadership, courage, malice, wrath, rage

Pink: Sensitivity, emotionality, femininity, longing, softness

Orange: Active intelligence, self-confidence, joy, happiness, warmth

Orange-red: Desire, pleasure, thirst for action, idealism, pride, vanity

Orange-yellow: Sharpness, intellect, self-confidence, industriousness

Gold: Transformation, dynamic energy, inspiration, devotion

Yellow: Intellect and mind, talent for organization, discipline, ego

Light yellow: Openness, ease, clear intellect, strong personality, freshness

Green: Love, growth, change, nature, rest, neutrality

Yellow-green: Sympathy, compassion, peacefulness, frankness

Dark green: Adaptability, cunning, deceit, materialism

Blue: Introversion, rest, coolness, solitude, truth, devotion, inner peace, wisdom

Indigo: Healing ability, kindness, reticence, seriousness, caution, integrity

Turquoise: Loving, healing aspect of the heart, generosity of life, teaching

Lavender: Mysticism, magic, profoundness, intolerance, psychic abilities

Violet: Intuition, art, creativity, faith, imagination, reticence, mysteriousness

Magenta: Spiritually perceptive

White: Spirituality, oneness, open to channeling

◆ ◆ ◆

MORE OF CHRISTINA'S THOUGHTS

❖ Go to the supermarket early in the morning, when it is quiet. The aisles are empty, and there are no lines at the cashier. Make it an enjoyable time for yourself, instead of going during rush hour and getting frustrated by the crowds.

❖ Stop drinking caffeine. This is a big one! We are truly lucky to have decaffeinated coffee that has the same great taste as regular coffee. I never thought I would give it up, but one day, I switched to decaffeinated coffee and I felt a huge difference. When you are excited about your life, you don't need stimulants. The energy comes from that peaceful place within.

❖ If you are divorced, take time to work on yourself before getting involved in another relationship. If you don't, you will repeat the same pattern and attract a similar type of relationship. You might

feel lonely at times, but if you take time to know yourself, you will grow and attract the right person and you will be happier in the long run because you would have found your own soul. Rent the movie *Under the Tuscan Sun*, if you have not seen it yet. Do something that inspires you. It may be hard to think of yourself after you have been married, but that's the time to figure out who you are.

❖ Always remember that we reap what we sow. So come on, write your goals and get started. You are lucky to have so many tools available for you. Why not use them for evolution?

❖ Wear nice lingerie for yourself, not just for your partner.

❖ I agree with the Buddhist philosophy that we should live in the moment; however, we should have goals as well. The mystery here is to try to balance the two. I found myself letting go for a while and living one day at a time and, other times, I thought seriously about my goals. You have to know when to push for your goals and when to let the universe handle them for you.

❖ Be aware if you are eating a lot. Ask yourself, *Why am I eating like this? What am I hungry for? What am I missing?* This will help you to stop the negative pattern and think about what you really need to fill your soul.

❖ Lao Tsu's secret of long life and lasting vision
   was described in Shakespeare's *Henry VI*:

   "My crown is in my heart not on my head;
   Not decked with diamonds and Indian stones,
   Nor to be seen:
   My crown is called content:
   A crown it is that seldom kings enjoy."

   Please remember this.

❖ I received this Chinese proverb by email but I do
   not know its author:

   If you want happiness for an hour, take a nap
   If you want happiness for a day, go fishing
   If you want happiness for a month, get married
   If you want happiness for a year, inherit a fortune
   If you want happiness for a lifetime, help others

❖ Pick a noun or verb that you want to understand better and look it up in a thesaurus. It is
   a great way to expand your vocabulary and, at
   the same time, to find out how that word can
   lead to another, which will guide you to a deeper
   understanding.

   Example: self-realization = self-fulfillment
                              = self-understanding
                              = self-awareness
                              = self-achievement

Transformation of consciousness

$\qquad$ = of perception

$\qquad$ = of awareness

$\qquad$ = of realization

❖ Do the following exercise periodically:

My intention: (State what you want to accomplish)

My attention: (State what you are going to do about it)

Manifestation: (Accomplishing what you have set out to do)

EXAMPLE:

My intention: To save money

My attention: Look at the household expenses and see where I can cut corners

Manifestation: Some extra savings in the bank

❖ List everything you have learned from your romantic relationships. Do you see a pattern of similarities or do you see differences?

❖ List five things that you lose yourself in while doing.

❖ List five things that come to you naturally.

❖ List five traits in your personality that you are proud of. What can you do to become a better person?

❖ List five things that you are passionate about.

❖ List three subjects that always come to your mind.

❖ List five things that you would like to accomplish during your life on Earth.

❖ List five things that relax you.

❖ List five things that will enhance your life.

❖ List names of people who have hurt you in the past, and find it in your heart to forgive them.

❖ Notice when you are happy. What is happening? What are you doing?

❖ Notice when you are down. What is causing it?

❖ Notice when you are frustrated and angry. What is going on?

❖ Notice the things that energize you. Energy is positive because it means that you are in your spirit.

❖ Notice when you are smiling. What is making your lips stretch from one ear to the other? The more you do things to release your tension peri- odically, like taking care of yourself and nurtur- ing your soul, the more you will find yourself

smiling. Self-awareness is the key to changing what we don't like.

❖ What does living "in spirit" mean to you? Write what comes to your mind.

❖ The conditions that turn consciousness toward love are simple:

♥ Giving love to others and receiving it back
♥ Sitting alone in your own silence
♥ Immersing yourself in natural beauty
♥ Making art and appreciating it
♥ Telling the truth whatever the consequences
♥ Laughing, dancing, playing with a child
♥ Having an outlet for joy
♥ Communing with deep emotions
♥ Acting out of kindness and compassion
♥ Bonding, feeling at one with a group whose goals are positive
♥ Offering yourself in service

❖ The emotions of peace are:

♥ Compassion
♥ Understanding
♥ Love

❖ Peace offers the mind:

♥ Connection to spirit and to all
♥ Mature love

- ♥ Love of self
- ♥ Inner strength
- ♥ Fulfilled desires
- ♥ Achievement
- ♥ Giving
- ♥ Inspiration
- ♥ Vision

❖ Happiness comes from one's connection to God and the universe, wherever one is in the world.

❖ Money makes life easier and more enjoyable.

❖ Mother Teresa advised:

People are often unreasonable, irrational, and self-centered. Forgive them anyway. . . . Give the best you have, and it will never be enough. Give your best anyway.

❖ In the final analysis, it is between you and God. It was never between you and them anyway.

❖ Success is:

- ♥ Reaching one's highest potential
- ♥ Being passionate about life
- ♥ Following your dreams no matter what people tell you
- ♥ Perseverance and determination
- ♥ Giving back to the world and sharing your wealth

♥ Overcoming obstacles
♥ Having faith
♥ A balanced life
♥ Having a supportive family and network of friends
♥ Being grateful
♥ Humility
♥ Being a low-key millionaire

❖ Wholeness is:

♥ Balanced yin-yang (which means feminine/masculine characteristics)
♥ Oneness
♥ Freedom
♥ Joy, bliss, ecstasy
♥ Love
♥ Fulfillment
♥ Wealth
♥ Success
♥ Manifestation of prosperity
♥ Perfect health
♥ Ability to manage emotions
♥ Wisdom
♥ Waking up to your purpose
♥ Having intimate relationships

I'll be seeing you ♥♥♥

ABOUT THE AUTHOR

Christina Houri was born in Kuwait. She grew up in Lebanon, lived in Greece and France during the first part of the civil war in Lebanon, and then moved to New York City in 1981 at age fourteen. She attended the Lycée Français de New York until 1984, and after two years at Syracuse University, she transferred to the Fashion Institute of Technology in 1986, earning an AAS in fashion design. She did an apprenticeship in Paris for Maison Givenchy and later was a buyer at Colt Mercantile in New York City. She worked at Club Med in the French West Indies, the Bahamas, and Florida, which were formative years because she ran some of their boutiques and organized their fashion shows. While working at Le Jardin à l'Ouest, a French American preschool, as an assistant teacher, she learned she loved being around kids. She worked various jobs until, finally in 2006, she realized her dream of opening her own preschool in New York City. It was her pride and joy. Called Le Petit Paradis Preschool, it was a French bilingual two-classroom school based on Montessori and Bank Street philosophies and one of the first green preschools in New York City.

Christina passed away on August 19, 2014. She is survived by her father, Ibrahim Houri; mother, Elsi Hakim; and brother, Khalil Houri.

CPSIA information can be obtained at www.ICGtesting.com
Printed in the USA
BVIW12n0240190617
487247BV00006B/43